The Proper Care of
GUINEA PIGS

Peter Gurney

Guinea pigs are attractive and hardy little creatures that can make wonderful pets.

THE PROPER CARE OF GUINEA PIGS

All photos courtesy of the author, except as noted.

Special acknowledgment is given to Mrs. Vedra Stanley of the Cambridge Cavy Trust for her assistance in the preparation of the veterinary section of this book.

Distributed in the UNITED STATES by T.F.H. Publications, Inc., One T.F.H. Plaza, Neptune City, NJ 07753; in CANADA to the Pet Trade by H & L Pet Supplies Inc., 27 Kingston Crescent, Kitchener, Ontario N2B 2T6; Rolf C. Hagen Ltd., 3225 Sartelon Street, Montreal 382 Quebec; in CANADA to the Book Trade by Macmillan of Canada (A Division of Canada Publishing Corporation), 164 Commander Boulevard, Agincourt, Ontario M1S 3C7; in ENGLAND by T.F.H. Publications, PO Box 15, Waterlooville PO7 6BQ; in AUSTRALIA AND THE SOUTH PACIFIC by T.F.H. (Australia) Pty. Ltd., Box 149, Brookvale 2100 N.S.W., Australia; in NEW ZEALAND by Ross Haines & Son, Ltd., 82 D Elizabeth Knox Place, Panmure, Auckland, New Zealand; in the PHILIPPINES by Bio-Research, 5 Lippay Street, San Lorenzo Village, Makati, Rizal; in SOUTH AFRICA by Multipet Pty. Ltd., P.O. Box 35347, Northway, 4065, South Africa. Published by T.F.H. Publications, Inc. Manufactured in the United States of America by T.F.H. Publications, Inc.

Contents

Beautiful Beasties

"The most wonderful animals in the world!" I usually reply, when strangers ask what the creatures are that I have cradled in my lap, in the park.

If I am asked to be a little more specific and less general, I tell them it is a guinea pig, a rodent, and their enthusiasm usually wanes a little. However, when I point out that one of the guinea pig's nearest relations is the chinchilla, the eagerness to get acquainted returns.

Children especially are easily charmed by these lovable animals. Caring for a guinea pig pet can foster a child's sense of responsibility.

A cute face—including the teddy bear-like nose and pert little ears—is but one of the assets of these popular pint-sized pets.

Rodent, for most people, means rat, which does not have a very good press, though in my own experience, all the members of that denigrated species that I have met have been very convivial characters!

THE PET GUINEA PIG

As a pet, for child or adult, guinea pigs have everything going for them. They are a

One of the author's thirty-seven guinea pigs enjoying the sights and sounds of London. Guinea pigs are adaptable and are equally at home in the city or the country.

comfortable armful for a child, or a generous handful for an adult.

As can be gathered from my opening sentence, they are very portable, though strangely enough, not many people take them further afield than their gardens. I wouldn't dream of going out into a public park without my shopping basket carrying a couple of guineas. They are delightful company, and I have yet to find a better agent at making strangers into friends, for formality seems so out of place when people are mutually petting such a cuddly creature as a guinea pig.

They are practically odourless, their

herbivorous diet being one reason for this, the other, being their cat-like grooming behaviour.

They seldom bite, and providing they are handled regularly from about six weeks of age, their docility makes nonsense of their reputation for nervousness. In my opinion, these are the most "user friendly" pets available.

They are cheap and easy to feed, living on a diet of cereal and vegetable matter. A

Guinea pigs are a "take everywhere" kind of pet and will appreciate the opportunity for an outing.

commercial mix of cereal can be bought at all pet stores, and most of the vegetable can be gathered in the wild or made up of the parts of vegetables we throw out as waste.

If, as I hope, by the end of this book I have persuaded more people to keep these charming creatures in their own living rooms, then they will soon discover the most rewarding facet of all to these pets. That is the sheer joy of observing them, from birth to death, as they live out their little lives, content with the home their human host has provided for them.

Compared to many other kinds of pets, the needs of the guinea pig are modest.

Guinea pigs, or cavies, are not native to Guinea. Rather, they are found in several regions in South America.

From the guinea pig's point of view, there are two other great advantages to its being kept indoors. It will not be subject to the vagaries of weather, and any health problems can be detected early on. "The earlier the diagnosis, the better the prognosis," is the golden rule in most guinea pig ailments.

I will be brief with the historical and scientific technicalities of the guinea pig, or cavy, as most serious breeders refer to it. This name is derived from the Latin, Caviidae, given to classify animals with short or no tails. In point of fact, there is a residue of a tail called the stump, which can be felt under the skin.

NOMENCLATURE

Cavia porcellus, pig-like cavy, is the scientific name of the species, but I prefer to call it by the name I knew it as when I was a child: guinea pig. Its native home is not Guinea, and it is in no way related to the pig, either the farmyard or the wild variety. The only thing it has in common with the pig is its habit of constantly rooting around for food on the ground, which is one of the reasons why it is sometimes referred to as the restless cavy. The other reason is its well-known habit of sometimes sleeping with its eyes open.

Its native home is the mountains and grasslands of several countries in South America, where in some regions it is regarded as a food.

It arrived in England in the middle of the seventeenth century, a little while after it had reached Europe. In most European countries that have coastlines, it is called a sea pig, derived from the fact that the sailors

This handsome guinea pig exhibits the alert, attentive nature of his species.

Guinea pigs that are housed indoors are not subject to the discomfort of unpleasant weather conditions. Additionally, they are safe from predators.

little pig of India.

There has been much debate in guinea pig circles about the derivation of the English name for the animal. It could be because the English sailors went round the Cape and returned to England via New Guinea, which accounted for the first part of its name. An alternate theory is that because of its rarity at that time, it was of great value. A guinea, sterling, was the going rate for it. This would have been a huge sum in those days, when an average yearly wage would have been about eight pounds!

The pig part of the animal's name could have been chosen

brought it in. Oddly enough, Italy, which has one of the longest coastlines of all, uses the charming name of porcellino da India, because of the grunts and squeals the guinea pig makes, or simply because it is short legged in relation to its body's length and depth, and its head and shoulders merge, in appearance at least, "necklessly," as does a pig's.

GUINEA PIGS IN GENERAL

The two favourite occupations of guinea pigs are sleeping and eating, and for the latter, they are equipped with teeth well suited for the task. There are two pairs of chisel-sharp incisors, set well forward to the front of the jaws, which are used for gnawing and biting off small portions of food. The

The front of a guinea pig's head is blunt in appearance. A good specimen of a guinea pig will have a snout that is fairly broad.

single pair of premolar teeth and three pairs of molars grind the hard grains, seeds and grasses that are the mainstay of their diet. These teeth are set so far back in their jaws that many people are surprised that they even exist.

The forefeet have four toes while the back have three, though it is not unusual for a fourth claw, which is very similar to a dog's dew claw, to grow. The guinea pig's feet are also padded like a dog's, making the animal very firm footed. The guinea pig has a low centre of gravity and can move about at high speed with firm stability.

The guinea pig wears a coat of hair, not fur. This coat can vary in colour, length and texture, according to the types of breed, which are now many more in number than the original breeds in the wild.

The animal's eyesight is poor, but its hearing is good. Its sense of smell, in my experience, ranges from acute to poor. However, whatever a guinea pig's olfactory abilities may be, that nose remains, for me, one of the most engaging of all its physical assets. With the line of its split upper lip, below the flair of its delicate nostrils, it always reminds me of a

Guinea pigs do not have a keen sense of vision, but their hearing is good.

The author and his guinea pig Free Range Fred, who, as his name implies, has complete run of the house.

to three pounds for a sow, and three to three and a half pounds for a boar. However, the animals that fall below this average, some going as low as two pounds, can be just as healthy and make just as good pets.

Guinea pigs are the least prolific of all rodents. This is partly due to the long term of pregnancy when compared with most other rodents. They produce two to three young in the first litter, then four to six in subsequent pregnancies.

lovingly stitched "Y" upon the face of a child's dearly cherished teddy bear.

The average weights of healthy pet guinea pigs are two and a half

The ailments that guinea pigs suffer from are similar to those that human flesh is heir to, and a few that are species specific. I have always looked upon this fact as an advantage, for it means that many of the drugs and treatments that are prescribed for humans can be used upon guinea pigs, with one or two exceptions.

As is the case with many other domestic animals, the guinea pig's life span is much dependent upon the standard of care its owner is prepared to provide. It used to be four to five years, but I believe that five to seven years can now be expected, in the light of improved husbandry and veterinary care.

Though I have no professional qualifications, running a guinea pig refuge, as

There are four toes on the guinea pig's front feet and three on the back. The soles of the feet are amply padded.

I do, using my own limited resources, has made it a sheer necessity to do most of the veterinary work myself. There are some conditions under which it is essential to seek professional advice and have the patient treated with prescription-only drugs. I have a vet who is very good with small animals, and I strongly advise owners to seek out such vets for themselves.

When I show the owners of the guinea pig patients I treat just how much can be done for their animals by themselves, they are amazed and touchingly grateful. I'm well aware of the reason for that gratitude. I know only too well the intense

The first litter of a guinea pig ranges from two to three in size. This number increases—from about four to six—in subsequent litters.

Following the basics of good animal husbandry can help to ensure that your guinea pig is a healthy and happy pet.

feeling of pride when you can look at a guinea pig that has recovered its health through your own intervention and can say to yourself "I did that!"

Getting people to take on this veterinary work bonds them even closer to their animals, and experience has taught me that it can mean the difference between life and death for a guinea pig.

Good husbandry is, of course, key to everything. The better it is, the less those veterinary skills will be called upon.

A Home of Their Own

There are three important factors, which are sometimes overlooked, to consider when providing guinea pigs with homes. One is the likelihood of the need for expansion.

The habit of keeping guinea pigs is extremely addictive, and only those with the strongest of wills can resist the temptation to have yet more!

This well-equipped outdoor hutch provides ample room for its occupants. Note the canvas on top, which can readily be rolled down in inclement weather.

The second factor is the ease of access for servicing. Indoors or out, the accommodation will have to be cleaned out two to three times a week, and even the everyday chores of feeding and watering can be made easier with a little bit of forethought.

Thirdly, provision should be made to guard against predators. I am not only talking about the stray dog that happens to leap the garden wall. The ones I have in mind are the "friendly, wouldn't harm a fly" little household muts, especially those with terrier in their lineage!

The sight of a beastie in a box can bring the

A mirrored living area will keep a guinea pig occupied some of the time.

average pet dog's wild hunting instincts surging to the surface. Denied of its prey, its frustration can drive it to feats of salivating

A guinea pig quenching his thirst. Water bottles such as those pictured here are ideal watering devices. There is no way that the animal can soil the water.

savagery. I know of one particular case where one of these unfortunate dogs ended up with bad lacerations to its muzzle and broken teeth as a result of tearing at the wire-mesh front of a guinea pig hutch. The guinea pigs within had the sense to retreat to the sleeping compartment, but the experience played havoc with their nervous systems for some weeks after the incident!

Be fair to your dog, and protect your stock by keeping temptation well out of reach by locating the accommodation at least three feet off the ground—on well-anchored legs or secured against a wall or sturdy fence.

THE OUTDOOR HUTCH

The outdoor hutch should be made of tongue-and-groove flooring that is at least half an inch thick. The roof must be weather proofed with roofing felt, be slanted away from the wire-mesh front, and overlap the rear of the hutch by at

Free Range Fred "visiting" a sow. If you do not want to take on the responsibility of raising a guinea pig family, males and females should be housed separately.

least two inches. This is to prevent the rain from dripping in through the two one-inch-diameter holes that should be drilled high up on the back of the hutch to facilitate ventilation.

The overall dimensions should be three to four feet in length by at least eighteen inches depth, and twenty inches in height. Ideally, the whole of the front of the hutch should be hinged so that it will fall downward for ease of access when cleaning.

Hinged to the leading edge of the bottom of the hutch should be a wooden shutter that can be pulled up over the front at night or in bad weather.

Alternatively, a detachable shutter can be fitted, or a canvas or heavy plastic cover, which can be rolled down when necessary, could be attached to the roof.

About a third of the way along the inside of the hutch a partition should be fitted. This can either have a small access-archway cut in the centre, or it can be brought up short of the back of the hutch to permit access that way. This compartment is where the door section of the front of the hutch should be fitted.

Hutches that are housed under a lean-to need not be quite as sturdy, but the rules about height, firm

Guinea pigs, like other rodents, have a proclivity for gnawing. Don't let your pet have access to anything that you wouldn't want him to chew on.

Guinea pigs are generally hardy animals, but they should not be subjected to extreme changes in temperature.

I would still advise the rule about height to be observed, for even if your dog is banned, doors can be left open by mistake. A dog would regard such an occurrence as an open invitation to drop in for a "take-away!"

It is important that the shed be weatherproof but well ventilated. Without a good air-flow, dampness will quickly build up in wintertime, and in summer it will become stiflingly hot. As guinea pigs are susceptible to respiratory infections under cold conditions, and heat exhaustion under hot conditions, just any old shed will not do.

anchorage, and security still apply.

If the guinea pigs are going to be accommodated in a shed, then the scope of design widens considerably. However,

The hutches or pens

in a shed can be made of thin plywood, and the sleeping compartments can be made of an up-turned wooden box with one side cut away.

INDOOR ACCOMMODATIONS

For years, pet shops have stocked a variety of cages that comfortably accommodate guinea pigs. Most come

It goes without saying that a guinea pig outdoors can be subject to a number of dangers. Use extra caution in this regard.

equipped with a sliding bottom compartment (for ease in cleaning) as well as food and water containers.

I now get onto my hobbyhorse by blatantly promoting what I consider to be the best accommodation of all, and that is in the comfort of your own home. It is here that the options for types of accommodation are almost endless.

I live with thirty-seven guinea pigs in a small flat, and I do not suffer from any of the following: unsightly hutches, bad odours, hay-strewn carpets, or a huge hole in my bank balance caused

Bedtime for Free Range Fred. Guinea pigs are diurnal animals, which means that they are most active during the daytime.

If you want to pamper your pet, you can provide him with a soft rug upon which he can rest, but it really isn't necessary to do this.

by some kind of super-elaborate accommodation I have constructed.

The pens that house my guinea pigs have been made out of old building material. Only the lighting was bought new—and that can be an optional extra.

By far, the easiest pens that I made are those that are tiered five high in my kitchen. They are simply the drawers from various sets of drawers that I have salvaged from builder's scrap skips. It is a very simple matter to cut one side away, then insert a length of glass. Old shop-display shelves are ideal for this purpose, for they come with already bevelled edges. Line the bottom with a piece of linoleum, and there you have a perfect guinea pig home!

If there are no cats or dogs around to have designs on your stock, then this kind of pen can be set down on the floor. It's a good idea to fit castors on the pen for ease of mobility.

The height of these pens should be about ten inches. Though there have been a couple of occasions when one of my boars has managed to get itself over and into a pen of this height, the traffic has never gone the other way. I put this down to the fact that the pen contained the irresistible lure of twelve sows to tempt him in and not a lot on my side of the pens to tempt them out!

The only accessories that I have in my pens are the food troughs or bowls and drip-feed drinking bottles. I don't even provide the highly recommended logs of wood for them to gnaw upon. In my experience, even a fresh piece of log gets only the most derisory of nibbles, and after a day, it is almost totally ignored.

Guinea pigs are not the kind of animals that play with toys or run around exercise wheels. As for boxes or fixed sleeping compartments, which I was told were essential, when I was green in the ways of guinea pigs, indoors they are unnecessary.

Indoor guinea pigs have to get used to the human company about the place, and if there is a bolt hole to scurry to each time a human comes blundering into the room, they will never really settle. It isn't fair to them, and it does little for the self-esteem of the owner if every time he or she enters the room his guinea pigs run away and hide.

After a while, new guinea pigs soon realise that there is a division between their territory and the

By nature, the guinea pig is a curious creature who can be quite mischievous.

human's, and this gives them a sense of security. I am always complimented on the tameness of my guinea pigs, and though I probably handle them more than most other guinea pig owners handle their pets, I

Guinea pigs are not particularly agile climbers, but they can move about fairly speedily.

depth. At each end of the main pen I have gradients of granite steps, one leading up to the drinking bottles, and one to the main food trough.

Sometime in the future, I intend to make a rockery in the corner of the room and install half bricking in the surrounding area to make a snug little guinea pig living area.

I think the scope for this kind of accommodation is endless. It's open to individual tastes and purses, and the only thing to be born in mind, after the comfort of the guinea pigs and the aesthetic value, is the convenience of servicing it.

For many years I

think the main reason for their docility is my kind of open-plan housing. (Some other hobbyists might hold a different view on the matter of using boxes and sleeping compartments, but, again, I maintain that they are not needed.)

The walls of some of my pens are mirrored, which gives them more kept my stock on a bedding of wood shavings, but about a year ago I switched to hay. This switch wasn't because of the scorn some breeders of guinea pigs pour upon the wood shavings, for I have never come

A Coronet guinea pig and a Rex guinea pig. Guinea pigs can be susceptible to heatstroke, so don't overdo your pet's "sunbathing."

Guinea pigs cannot adapt to damp and/or cold conditions, which can cause respiratory problems. Therefore, they should not be allowed outdoors unless the weather is pleasant.

across a health problem that I could attribute to using this kind of bedding material. It was simply that my supply began to deteriorate, becoming dusty, and I managed to get a cheap supply of hay to use instead, which I found made the task of cleaning far easier.

I line the bottom of my pens with newspaper, which I

Guinea pig pals. Watching the interaction between a pair of guinea pigs is interesting and enjoyable.

then cover with a layer of hay. All I have to do when the pens become soiled after two or three days is to roll up the newspaper with the hay and droppings enclosed. Newspaper is absorbent enough to cope with the small amount of urine that guinea pigs pass.

Shredded paper can also be used as a bedding, but the bottom lining of newspaper will still be necessary. Straw must never be used, for the guinea pig's habit of rooting around at ground level makes its eyes extremely

essential food, not only as roughage but as a teeth-grinding agent.

I have a guinea pig who goes by the name of Free Range Fred, and his name gives a

Guinea pigs need a safe, secure spot to which they can retire. When your guinea pig is resting, do not disturb him.

vulnerable to the hard stems. Eye injuries in stock kept on straw are very common! Straw is also not edible, whereas hay is an

clue to the other way that a guinea pig can be housed. He does none other than live in my flat, though he has got his own private

A lovely Dutch guinea pig. Its colouration and markings resemble that of the Friesian cow and the Dutch rabbit.

quarters to retire to when he has had enough of me! These quarters are a bottom drawer, with the front cut away, of a record and cassette storage cabinet.

In my experience, there are two factors that qualify a guinea pig to fully cohabit with a human: it should be a boar and it should not gnaw!

On the whole, guinea pigs do not gnaw as much as most other rodents, and in their own specially built homes it doesn't matter if they do or not. However, apart from adding a new form of finely nibbled decorative art to your most expensive piece of furniture (they

An assortment of young guinea pigs. Never leave a guinea pig in a place from which it could fall and injure itself.

If you keep a pair of guinea pigs, it is most likely that they will form a closer attachment with each other than with you.

invariably go for the best), it can be a matter of life or death if they roam freely in your home. A live electric cable can be just as appealing to a guinea pig as is your favourite piece of furniture, and electrocution is an unpleasant way to exit! If you do decide to give your pet free access to your home and it nibbles at things during the first few days, persevere. As with the case of the gnawing logs, interest usually wanes with familiarity. However, it is a good idea to cover, or re-route to a higher level, electric cables.

The reason I maintain that a boar makes a better flat-mate than a sow is that I felt that the several sows I did try to cohabit with just didn't seem to be happy with the arrangement. They would immediately scurry away to their own quarters when I entered the room and were always agitated whenever they got close to the main pen—obviously longing to be in with some sister pigs.

Perhaps the sows would have been more happy if I had been a woman. I do know of one lady who had a free-range sow that was extremely convivial, but as there were no other guinea pigs to distract her, this is not cast-iron proof that sows will settle for people rather than pigs!

Fred obviously takes a keen interest in the sows behind the glass front of their pens, but his interest is purely sexual. He is quite content to lie with his nose pressed up against the glass and admire the "goodies" for a short time. However, he soon gets bored and begins to scurry about the flat, exploring all his

After playtime outdoors, a short-haired guinea pig requires hardly any grooming, but a long-haired guinea pig will need a thorough going-over.

favourite nooks and crannies or simply settling down for a snooze in them.

He is practically house trained, confining most of his droppings to his own quarters. There are the occasional "mishaps" but they are few and far between, and I take the attitude of "what's a few pellets between friends!"

A word of warning though! It is advisable to put notices about the place, such as mine, which state, "Watch out, watch out, Fred's about!" Before these signs were put up, he was trod on, kicked and even nearly thrown out with the rubbish! Doors are the other hazard, and I never close one behind me without first checking that Fred's head or bottom is out of range. I open all doors extremely cautiously, just in case friend Fred is on the other side.

One final word on

An Abyssinian guinea pig. Abyssinians are distinguished by the rosettes, or whorls, of hair on their bodies.

Guinea pigs are small animals, and if they are allowed to run loose in your home they can easily be trampled. All human members of the household should be mindful of this fact.

housing. No matter where you may have read that they make good companions, rabbits and guinea pigs should never share accommodation.

An increasingly common cause of death in guinea pigs is rabbits. Just watch how many times a rabbit kicks back with its powerful rear legs as it hops about the place. If those legs connect with a guinea pig's ribs or kidney, it has little chance of survival.

Which One Shall It Be?

Compared with the wide range of variety in the canine world, that of the guinea pig is far less cluttered and diverse. The various breeds are distinguished by bracketing them into long, short, and rough haired and then sub-dividing them by coat colours, or combinations of colours and hair textures.

Body weight between breeds varies very little. As far as temperament, though people who specialise in breeding or fancying

Below and facing page: There is a wide variety of guinea pigs from which you can choose...Something for everyone.

one particular breed may take issue with me here, in my own experience, temperament is seldom predictable by breed.

ABOUT THE BREEDS

"Selfs" have short-haired coats of one colour all over, and there are about ten colours in the officially recognised English Self.

The marked, short-coated guinea pigs have names that are fairly self-explanatory.

The Dalmatian's colouration is similar to that of the dog of that name. The Tortoiseshell's is like that of the tortie-marked cat. The Roan's colour is like that of the roan horse, while the Dutch is marked like the Dutch Friesian cow.

The White comes in dark- and ruby-eyed varieties. The Himalayan's colouration is like that of the Himalayan rabbit. It has a dark nose and feet, either black or chocolate.

There are only two types of rough-haired guinea pigs, and they are the Crested and the Abyssinian. The Crested sports an attractive rosette around the top of its head, which gives it a jaunty appearance. The rosette of the English Crested is the same colour as the rest of the coat, while that of the American has a bit more of the razzle-

This is an English Crested guinea pig, so named for the rosette atop its head. In English Cresteds, the colour of the rosette and the rest of the body are the same. In the American Crested, the center of the rosette is white.

dazzle to it—the interior of it is white, which gives it a bright contrast to the rest of the coat.

Abyssinians have rosettes all over their bodies, but they have to be a specific number and in a set pattern to qualify as a purebred.

The Silver Agouti sports a coat of the colour and tone that typifies the dress of most guinea pigs in the wild. There are also Lemon, Golden, Cinnamon and Salmon varieties. The sheen of the Agouti coat is caused by the tips of the hair shafts being many times lighter than that of the shaft of the hair itself.

A Black Self guinea pig. When an animal is described as a self, it simply means that its colour is the same all over its body.

The three basic types of guinea pig coat are: long, short, and rough. Within these three categories, there exist a number of colours and colour combinations.

My own particular favourites are the long-haired varieties, and there are three of these: the Peruvian, the Sheltie and the Coronet.

In the Peruvian, the hair of the coat grows towards the animal's head, while in the Sheltie and the Coronet, it flows backwards. The added feature of the Coronet is a rosette of hair, similar to that of the Crested, on the top of its head.

There is one other breed that is classified by its silky coat and this is the Satin.

These, then, are the main breeds, but there are a few offshoots and relative rarities, two of which are the Rex, which is known in America as the Teddy, and the Texel. Both have frizzy coats. The Rex's hair is short, and the Texel's is long. The Rex is more common than the Texel, but both are rapidly expanding in numbers.

As far as "less than perfect" specimens are concerned, I want to "tell it as it is," so to

A Himalayan guinea pig. This attractive colour pattern also appears in several other kinds of animals.

An Abyssinian guinea pig. Each rosette on an Abyssinian should be sharply defined and radiate from a distinct center point. The coat is rough and wiry in appearance.

speak, for the majority of guinea pig life in most countries where they are kept as pets. I hasten to add that there is no element of inverted snobbery in my motivation. I love to see and handle a nice broad-snouted, wide-bodied show pig with the best of them. However, the "mongrel" guinea pig is as worthy of our admiration and love as those that conform to the exacting standards of

An inquisitive Coronet guinea pig. No matter what kind of guinea pig you choose, you will love your little pet for his amusing ways.

national cavy associations.

If your pet shop dealer doesn't stock the particular breed of guinea pig that you want, perhaps he can order it for you or refer you to a breeder.

HOW MANY?

An important consideration is the number of guinea pigs that are required. Remember that they are pack animals, enjoying the company of their own kind. It is always kindest to take at least a pair, except if you are intending to have a free-range boar. There is no more effort required to house and care for two than there is for one.

It is certainly not a good idea to have a boar and a sow right from the start. They will, of course, breed, which will mean reorganising your housing arrangements soon after to accommodate the baby boars and sows, which

Simon and Garfunkel, Buff Selfs who are brothers. Garfunkel (facing front) is a fine example of his breed. His head is generously broad, his eyes are well spaced, and his nose is Roman. Simon is on the smaller side, and his coat is a bit thin in certain parts.

obviously have to be separated.

I hold to the view that giving away guinea pigs because a little forethought was not given to controlling their population is to be discouraged. Responsible owners should care about the offspring of their stock and breed only when there is certainty about good homes being available.

A Cream Self guinea pig. A pet-quality pig is equally as lovable as a show-quality pig.

Remember that, as a general rule, two boars will only live together peacefully if they have been brought up together or a young one has been introduced to an adult and then grown up with it.

Preferably, your first guinea pigs should be between six and eight weeks of age. An average weight for a guinea pig of this age would be eight to ten ounces, and it should be between five and six inches in length.

HOW TO CHOOSE

The advice usually given when choosing puppies is to avoid the ones that sit on their own and always favour the ones that run to you. A guinea pig invariably runs and hides at the approach of any stranger, but this is the sign of a guinea pig showing healthy caution. Take your time and observe them for a couple of minutes or so, and watch for the first one to poke its nose out and give you a nasal

Tortoiseshell guinea pigs. Take your time when you make your selection: observe your prospective pet carefully.

A Silver Agouti guinea pig. Be sure to check the condition of the skin and coat, which is a good indicator of the animal's general state of health.

The point I'm trying to make is that choosing a guinea pig is nothing like choosing a dog. Personally, I always go for the loners, for in my experience, they usually turn out to be more at ease with humans. However, even these quiet ones should scurry away in great haste at any attempt to pick them up when they are young.

The primary indicators of the health of a guinea pig are its skin and coat condition. Beware of those with a thinning of the coat, or those who have small bald patches surrounded by broken hair shafts, as this would be

sizing up! It is just as likely to be the quiet one that was sitting in the corner, who will be just as healthy as its more boisterous companions.

A Rex guinea pig. (In the U.S., this breed is known as the Teddy.) Rexes are distinguished by their short frizzy coats.

indicative of a fungal or parasitic infestation. Run your fingers through the coat, especially around the rump, under the jaws and around behind the ears. These are the areas that receive puncture wounds as the result of fighting. If you find one, move the hair away from the site with the tips of your fingers and check that there is no inflammation. If there is just a small scab that is healing cleanly, or one or two scars, this could be a plus in choosing the animal, for it probably means that its immune system is a good one.

The nose should be dry, and there should be no catarrhal sounds. The eyes should be bright and clear. There should be no waxiness in the corner of the eyes nearest to the snout.

The short-haired breeds are the most common, followed closely by the rough, especially the Abyssinian. For a long time, I avoided the long-haired breeds, thinking that they would require much

A Dalmatian guinea pig, named after the breed of dog that exhibits a similar colouration. If you are interested in showing your guinea pig, you should be fully acquainted with the standard for his breed.

Long-haired guinea pigs don't necessarily mean a lot of extra work on your part. Regularity in their grooming schedule is the key in keeping them looking their best.

more grooming. I have since learned that this is not the case, so do not be deterred by all those luscious locks!

The golden, and most frustrating, rule of early guinea pig ownership is to leave them alone when once you have them home. Their new home, strange environment, and, above all, new

A guinea pig patiently awaiting dinnertime. Your guinea pig's feed and water bowls should be non-tippable.

or spend too much time by their accommodation. This will only prolong that settling-in period. Content yourself with feeding and watering them, and cleaning out their quarters.

FEEDING GUIDELINES

The feeding of guinea pigs is a relatively simple matter, providing you keep two things in mind. One is that, like us, guinea pigs cannot manufacture their own vitamin C, like most other mammals do. Therefore, fresh vegetable matter is essential.

Secondly, it is important that guinea pigs are made to work

human companions are of unknown quality, and consequently, frightening to small, nervous animals. No matter how tempted you may feel, do not keep picking them up for their food as they do in the wild, where they have to grind down much roughage before they get sufficient nourishment. Mother Nature has equipped them with constantly growing teeth in order to cope with the tough wear and tear caused by their heavy workload.

New owners, and, sadly, some of those with long experience in keeping guinea pigs look askance at me when I advise that they take as much interest

A nutritionally balanced guinea pig diet will include regular amounts of roughage.

in the hardness of the food as they do in its protein value. It should be made up of bone meal, flaked pulses, hard grains, grass pellets and various seeds. Feed the molassed mixes only occasionally, to vary the diet.

The mistake that most people make, early on in their guinea pig-keeping career, is to assume that just because there seems to be a lot of a particular pulse or grain left untouched in the feed bowls that none is eaten. They then decide to make up a mix of the other parts of the food that apparently were more appreciated by their guinea pigs.

Firstly, though some particular part of the food may have been less popular than another, it doesn't follow that none was consumed. Close examination will reveal that what remains after eating is what appears to be a fine-grained powder. This will be the residue of the harder grains, which are usually those that are less popular. That powdery waste is evidence that they have been taken, and, consequently, the teeth have had to do some healthy hard grinding as they do in the wild.

Facing page: Bright clear eyes are one sign of good health in a guinea pig.

Secondly, you would not give to a child just the food that it preferred, and the same goes for young guinea pigs. It is not a kindness to allow them to develop lazy eating habits.

I certainly find myself doing more dental work on animals that have been fed on a mix made up by their owners than those that are fed on a commercial mix.

Another reason some people prefer to make up their own mixes is that they are mistakenly alarmed by what they consider to be the chemical additives listed on the labelling. They hold up their hands in horror when they see such words as phosphorous, selenium, copper and the like. "Oooh, nasty chemicals!" they cry.

In the wild, guinea pigs have easy access to items upon which they can gnaw. The domesticated guinea pig has to rely on his owner to meet this important need.

Commercial guinea pig food takes a lot of the guesswork out of what you should feed your pet. There are several varieties from which you can choose.

None of these are "nasty chemicals." They are essential elements in the normal healthy diet of humans as well as guinea pigs. They are either in the food naturally or have been added because they have been degraded in the processing.

Most rabbit mixes are fine, but there are a few on the market of which you should

A Sheltie guinea pig. Shelties, known as Silkies in the U.S., have a coat that is dense and silky in texture.

beware. They are the ones that have A.C.S. (Anti-Coccidiosis Spray) added. This is a medicine that protects rabbits against the condition, but it can harm the liver and kidneys of a guinea pig.

There is one other kind of great mix that is ideal for guinea pigs and that is one of the long-fibre herbal mixes for horses, which are obtainable in most countries that have stabled horses. These mixes are usually molassed but only lightly so. This is in addition to the guinea pig or rabbit mix.

These dry foods should be available all the time. I always ensure that my troughs and feed bowls remain topped up.

My guinea pigs twice weekly enjoy a treat that many vets and breeders will hold up their hands in horror at: a plate of brown bread and cow's milk. It is not the bread that

Guinea pigs do not manufacture their own vitamin C. Therefore, they must be fed vegetables and fruit that contain this vitamin.
Fresh food should not be left out for any great length of time, as it will spoil.

is objected to but the milk. I have yet to see a case of diarrhoea caused by this practice, and considering the usual longevity of my stock, there appears to be no long-term effects.

The vegetables, root crops, fruit and wild plants that are suitable for a guinea pig's diet are wide ranging. Practically all the vegetables we eat are ideal for guinea pigs. There are two that should not be overdone. They are spinach, because of its high oxalic acid content, and lettuce,

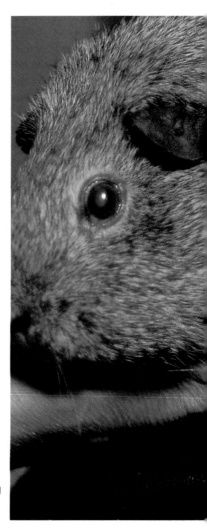

The average weight of a guinea pig is about three pounds. This figure can vary, depending on the breed.

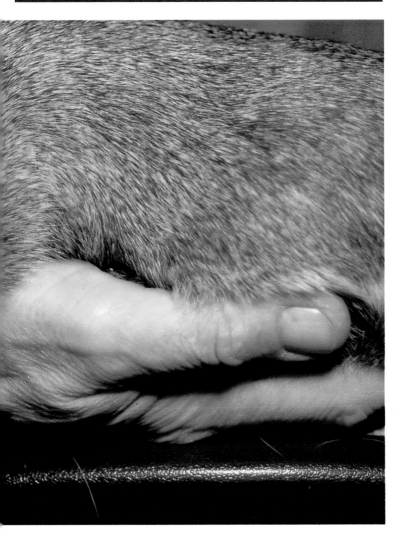

Every guinea pig is an individual with tastes and preferences all its own.

which contains laudanum and is of little food value.

Cauliflower leaves, kale, chicory, cabbage, spring greens, the list goes on and on, but don't expect each and every guinea pig to like each and every vegetable. Like us, they have their individual tastes. This is why it is essential to give as wide a choice as possible.

Most guinea pigs have a "Bugs Bunny" admiration of the noble carrot, and some are quite keen on beetroot. They will take a little parsnip and swede, but they are far from enthusiastic about them. They shouldn't be offered potatoes, for if there is any green in them it could prove toxic.

In the fruit line, they enjoy apples, pears,

Guinea pigs love to eat fresh grass. If you wish to indulge your pet with this dietary delight, make sure that the grassy area is clean and uncontaminated by chemicals and other animals' waste.

tomatoes, oranges, grapes and melons. There is a word of warning when it comes to feeding apples. Some guinea pigs have a weakness in the mouth membranes, which can be aggravated by the acid in apples, causing open sores in the corners of their mouths. Either cut the apples up into small cubes, rather than section them, or avoid feeding them at all to susceptible guinea pigs.

Hay that is used as bedding will be nibbled upon by your guinea pig. It should be fresh, dry, and free of any mold.

When introducing new foods to your guinea pig, do so gradually. This will lessen the likelihood of gastrointestinal problems.

All that I have mentioned above can cost money, though a lot of it can be provided by feeding the guinea pigs the parts of the food we throw away. I always regard bought food as a secondary, and I'm convinced that my guinea pigs do as well. What they prefer costs nothing at all and is very good for them. It is simply grass and all manner of wild plants.

One of the highlights of my year is when I feed my guinea pigs their first real crop of fresh spring grass. They fall upon it, purring with delight, and any of the cultivated vegetables are totally ignored—or left till last, whenever grass is available. Avoid grass at the side of roads: it could be contaminated by dogs and cats, and exhaust gasses from internal combustion engines can leave some nasty chemical on it. Municipal parks should also be avoided as a grass source, for most have been treated with weed killer.

It is a good idea to invest in a small wild-plants handbook that is well illustrated and warns of those plants that are toxic. The cost will be repaid in a very short time by extending the range of food you can gather in the wild, thus making savings on cultivated vegetables. The variation in diet will be greatly appreciated by your guinea pigs, and they will be healthier for it. The only rider I add is to play it safe: do not feed a plant that you are uncertain about.

EDIBLE PLANTS

Bramble—Remove thorny spine before

If you are going to let your guinea pig forage, be certain that he does not have access to poisonous plants. Investing in a handbook of wild plants is a good idea in this regard.

feeding.

Chickweed—Not a great deal of food value. Guinea pigs usually take only a little of this, but it adds that little bit of variety.

(A small point here about oversupplying

certain plants. In my experience, guinea pigs are remarkably adept at knowing what is good or not good for them. Plants that have powerful medicinal properties are always taken in small amounts.)

Coltsfoot—Very palatable to guinea pigs.

Dandelions—Easy with these as they have laxative qualities.

Groundsel—This is available practically all the year 'round. It too has laxative qualities, but it is taken only in small amounts.

Plantains—Rich in minerals and vitamins. Much enjoyed by guinea pigs, especially the young fresh leaves.

Shepherd's purse—

This is an excellent antidote to the scours (diarrhoea). Only very small amounts of it are eaten by a healthy guinea pig, but when it has the scours—and it is usually off all its green food on these occasions—it will eat this plant. A good example of a guinea pig knowing just what is good for it!

Vetches—These delicate little plants are devoured with great relish.

These are just a few of the excellent wild plants that are enjoyed by guinea pigs. The only proviso when gathering them is to leave out any that show any signs of fungal infestation on or under the leaves. This

A Coronet guinea pig. Some guinea pigs have larger appetites than others, but, in general, they do not "pig out."

shows up as a white powdery line, like tide marks, or orange clustering blotches.

With the proliferation of pesticide spraying in recent years, agricultural land should be avoided as sites for food gathering.

POISONOUS PLANTS

As a general rule of thumb, any plant grown from a bulb is usually toxic to a guinea pig. The list I give is of the more common poisonous plants. Some of these will no doubt come as a surprise to some people—they certainly did to me when I first became aware of them. Avoid: bracken, anemone, bluebell, buttercup, belladonna, celandine,

If you own several guinea pigs, you can let them have a community feed bowl, provided each animal gets his fair share.

Your guinea pig is a creature of habit and will be a happier and more contented pet if he has a regular daily routine.

convulvulus, docks, foxglove, monkshood, ragwort, and yew.

There are, of course, many more dangerous wild plants, but this shouldn't put the conscientious off. Foraging is fun, and the variety of food is good for the guinea pigs.

Guinea pigs are creatures of routine and habit, so establish set times for feeding vegetable matter: twice daily is advised. One of the pleasures of my day is the growing excitement of my guinea pigs' anticipating their meals at seven in the morning and five in the afternoon.

As for the amount to feed per guinea pig, I usually keep it to one handful at each feeding time.

To Have and To Hold

Most guinea pigs are nervous either because they have good reason to be, through bad handling, or because they have not been handled enough and consequently have not learned to trust their owners.

Hutched guinea pigs are the most difficult to tame up because the hand that comes in

When you first bring your guinea pig home, don't rush the acquaintance process. He needs time to get used to you and his new environment.

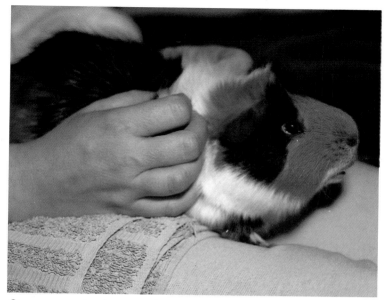

One sure way to win your guinea's trust and approval is to gently scratch and massage him, simulating the mutual grooming behavior of guinea pigs. Be sure to avoid the rump area, however, as guinea pigs do not like to be touched there.

to pick them up is regarded as invasive—obviously their enclosed quarters have more exclusivity than an indoor pen. However, though I believe these hutch-kept pigs can never be tamed as well as a house pig, much can be done if an effort to handle them as much as possible is made.

The first thing to learn is how to pick them up. Once the pair of you have gone

This is the safest way to put your pet back in his quarters: backwards. If you put him in head first, he may attempt to jump and can injure himself.

through the "statutory" hide-and-seek in the hay and you have pinned the pig down in a corner, slip your hand, palm uppermost, underneath it, and place the other on top. Be firm: the guinea pig will feel more secure when you lift it out.

HANDLING

Guinea pigs have an ostrich-like quality in that they bury their heads, if not in the sand, then in the corners of their quarters, when reached for by the human hand. Thus its rear end will probably be facing you. As soon

A guinea pig should be made to feel secure when he is being held. If you are nervous about holding your guinea pig, put him on a firm surface, such as a table, instead.

as you have it out, put it in your lap or on a firm surface and turn it around the other way, so that the nose faces up your arm and you cradle the rump in the palm of your hand. Always, always, place the other hand on the top of the guinea pig if you move around with

A guinea pig spends much time grooming itself. Sometimes it gets so enthusiastic in its efforts that it loses its balance and literally topples over!

With the hand on the top, the guinea pig feels more secure for the simple reason that it is! No matter how confident you may become, remember this rule. A sudden, strange noise is enough to start a guinea pig into flight, and it is a long way down from human-waist height!

GETTING ACQUAINTED

One of the best ways to get acquainted is to do something to the guinea pig that it likes doing to itself. One of its favourite occupations is grooming. Such is the guinea pig's enthusiasm for grooming, which it

it. From bitter experience, I well know the folly of not following this rule: it cost one of my guinea pigs its life when it fell to the ground!

Here is a grooming action that guinea pigs love: being scratched under the chin and behind the ears.

carries out using both its forepaws and its incisor teeth, that it sometimes falls over backwards! As it works its way down between its back legs, it becomes more ball shaped, and its quick, urgent actions can sometimes upset its equilibrium and over it goes!

This "getting to know you" kind of grooming is nothing like the brush-and-comb grooming of adult, or already acclimated, guinea pigs. Try that prematurely, and you will end up with a very angry guinea pig on your hands. What I am suggesting is a scratch and a massage that mimics the actions of guinea pigs' mutual grooming behaviour.

The area off-limits is

Some guinea pigs get very fidgety after being held for just a few minutes; other settle down and even fall asleep. If your guinea pig does not want to be held, don't force the issue.

This is a potentially dangerous situation: if the guinea pig is suddenly frightened, he could run in any direction, including into the pool. Use common sense when letting your pet loose outdoors.

the rump. Most guinea pigs are very intolerant of human fingers, or even their own kind, touching the lower back and the bottom. However, under the chin down onto the dewlap, around, under, and just behind the ears are the areas that one guinea pig will actually present to another to be nuzzled.

Some guinea pigs enjoy having the tops of their heads gently stroked with the tips of the fingers. Others hate it and violently throw their heads up in annoyance. Some people think this is cute and persist in

The sooner you introduce yourself to your pet, the sooner he will become accustomed to your touch.

Some young guinea pigs get very restless after a few minutes; others will quickly snuggle down into your lap and purr with delight or even snooze. Don't hang onto the restless ones—they will come around in their own good time.

From the very start, have plenty of nose-to-nose nuzzling! Guinea pigs value their noses highly. Their noses are their primary organ of introduction and social cementing! The "nasal nuzzle" is the guinea pig equivalent of the human handshake, but no matter how small and delicate you may regard your own nose, it is a little on the large side for a guinea pig! Your pet

doing it; don't!

All the time you are fondling the animal, talk to it softly. "Coochy coo" if you like. It's the tone of your voice that charms, not the intellectual content!

needs time to get used to it, so do not waste any—introduce yourself early on. It will pay dividends in the long run.

This close contact is as much for your own benefit as for the guinea pig's. I'm a firm

A guinea pig and his friends. You'll know you've won your guinea pig's trust when he lies contentedly when you pet him.

believer in the therapeutic benefits of stroking and fondling animals. Being uptight and feeling and hearing a guinea pig purr with appreciation at your touch at one and the same time is not possible! From the animal's point of view, not only will it feel more secure in your company, it will be more cooperative when you make medical checks on it. Thus its health will benefit. A struggling guinea pig does not aid diagnosis one little bit!

Occasionally, you will come across a guinea pig who will never become amenable to human

A guinea pig uses its sensitive nose to introduce itself...This "nasal nuzzle" is the guinea pig equivalent of a human's handshake.

If you are going to put your guinea pig back in its quarters head first, gently cup your hand over its face as you lower him down. Guinea pigs have been known to suffer broken front teeth and forelegs caused by their prematurely jumping down from their owner's hands.

handling, no matter how long you try to win it over. Respect its wishes and let it be. I have had a couple like this, but their wildness was, if anything, a plus, for it added a bright contrast to their more human-oriented peers.

When you put the

guinea pig back into its quarters, always put it in backwards, or cup your hand up over its face as you lower it down. The most common injuries to guinea pigs are broken front teeth and forelegs caused by the animals' jumping down into their quarters prematurely from their owner's hands.

Children should be told to always use the reverse method, for their hands are that much smaller.

Very young children should always be supervised when handling guinea pigs, and the older ones should be made aware that guinea pigs are far less robust than a dog, cat or rabbit.

HANDLING FOR GROOMING

I regard shampooing and grooming as much an exercise in preventive medicine as cosmetic procedure, but as these activities cannot be carried out without much handling I will deal with them in this chapter.

I shampoo all my stock at three-month intervals and groom them every couple of weeks or so—but more often if they are recovering from any kind of skin problems.

Most guinea pigs constantly shed hair in

Facing page: Bathtime. Few guinea pigs enjoy this experience, so try your best to carry out the procedure as quickly and efficiently as possible.

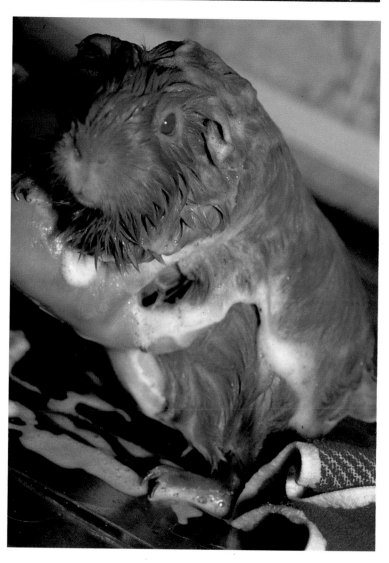

small amounts and sometimes at a greater rate. Strange as it may seem, it is the short-coated varieties that cast off the most hair. Occasionally, heavier hair loss can be caused by a skin infection—or even an internal problem. However, it's usually a natural process and no cause for alarm.

Guinea pigs are pretty good at combing

A squeaky-clean guinea pig. It is not necessary to bathe your pet more frequently than every three months or so.

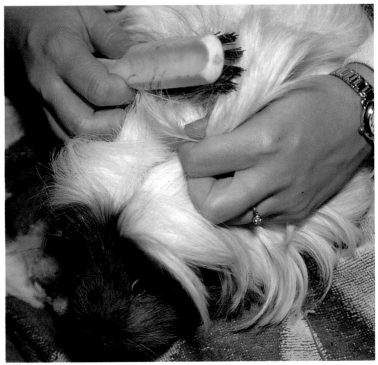

When you are de-knotting a long-haired guinea pig, firmly grasp the base of the hair shafts first—then brush or comb. This will prevent your tugging on the roots, which, of course, is uncomfortable for the animal.

out these hairs. I find them enchanting to watch as they diligently rummage with their forepaws, especially when they sit upright and get to work on their heads and whiskers. Their actions are just like those of a human washing its face—without benefit of face flannel.

An owner can actually encourage this grooming behaviour by brushing the coat from head to rump with a soft hairbrush. Never use a hard one, for the guinea pig has very sensitive skin. There is no doubt in my mind that most guinea pigs thoroughly enjoy this helping hand, though there are a few who most certainly do not. Most do not like it the first time but persevere. When first beginning this practice,

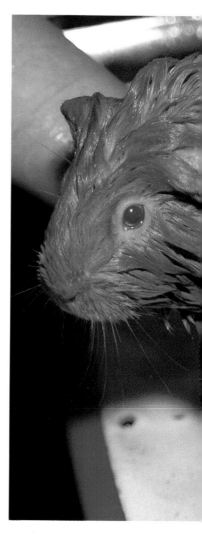

After lathering your pet, give him a thorough rinsing. Use a small container filled with water or hold the animal under the tap.

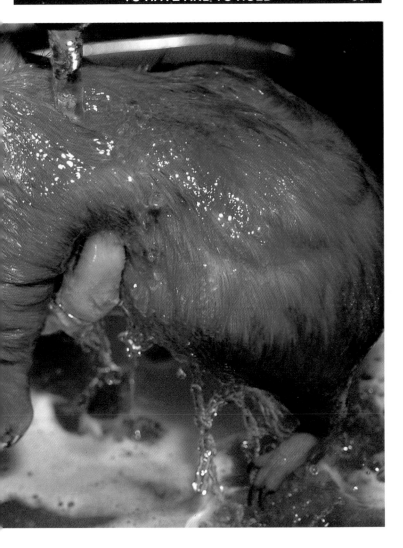

limit it to a few strokes of the brush, then gradually increase the amount of grooming each time you do it.

I prefer to do my short-haired guinea pigs with them sitting on my lap on a towel, but the long-haired guinea pigs are always placed on a firm surface at waist height.

The ends of the hair in the long-haired varieties can become knotted even if it is kept trimmed to a reasonable length. These cannot be combed or brushed out unless the animal has recently had a shampoo, when the

Towel dry your guinea pig to remove as much excess water as possible. Then you can use a hair dryer (set on low) on him or place him in a cardboard box with a hot water bottle at one end of it.

Grooming does more than help maintain your guinea pig's well-being: it strengthens the bond between you and him.

major part of the knotting can be much more easily teased out in the soapy water.

Shampooing is best done in a bowl that is placed in an empty bath, for guinea pigs quite enjoy spreading water around the place by shaking themselves like a dog emerging from swim, and it is amazing just how much water the coat can hold.

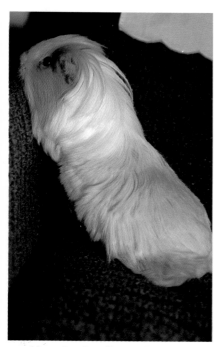

Many fanciers like to trim the hair of their long-haired guinea pigs. This little fellow sports a rag-mop style.

Fill the bowl to a depth of about three inches with warm water, and, ignoring all the high-decibel protests from the guinea pig about to be dunked (few enjoy the experience), place it in and soak it well. Once it is thoroughly wet, take it out and lather it up while it is standing in the bottom of the bath. Use one of the many mild animal-shampoos on the market that has anti-parasitic ingredients in it. The best way to hold a guinea pig while you are working the lather up is with the hand over the head, thumb and little finger holding the head steady while the other three fingers grip just behind the shoulders.

Don't be afraid to be quite vigorous with the hand working up the lather and rubbing it

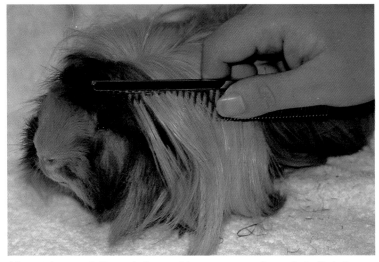

After a trim, comb through the coat to remove any loose hair. Pet shops stock a wide variety of grooming tools.

well in. To finish off around the head, neck and shoulders, position the guinea pig so that he is half standing up against the side of your side of the bath, facing you. Then work your way up. Some people find it's better to use both hands, while others use one, still holding the body of the guinea pig with the other. Naturally, you must avoid getting the soapy water in the guinea pig's eyes and nostrils, so have a small jug of warm water handy to rinse them clear.

A mild-formula coat conditioner is a nice finishing touch. It not only gives the coat a silky sheen but also transforms the guinea pig into a sweet-smelling, scampering pomander! This doesn't trouble the guinea pig in the slightest, and it can be positively beneficial when introducing new adult stock. The initial aggression of an established group toward a newcomer is

This guinea pig's hair has been layer cut right up to over its rump. The "look" of your pet's hairstyle is a matter of personal preference.

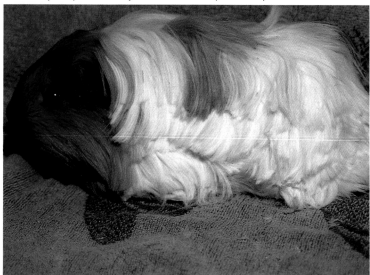

considerably decreased if its natural scent is suppressed by the fragrance of such grooming products.

I rinse my guinea pigs off by pouring a few jugs of warm water over them or holding them under a tap, after which I wrap them in a towel. I gather the long hair up in the folds of the towel and get the excess water off by using a hand rubbing-motion. The drying is completed by an electric hair dryer. Alternatively, the guinea pig can be put into a cardboard box with a hot water bottle placed at one end of it.

If it is an outdoor guinea pig, it is essential that it be thoroughly dried before it is returned to its quarters. A damp guinea pig is extremely susceptible to respiratory infections.

The time and effort that you devote to grooming will be more than compensated for by the pleasing appearance of your fluffy little pet.

The time it takes to complete the job is much dependent upon the guinea pig concerned. Some of the docile ones can turn out to be kicking, screaming maniacs when they are shampooed, while some of the wildest ones thoroughly enjoy the experience and are tranformed into gentle pussy cats as soon as they are lowered into the water.

Wait until the guinea

A Cream Self guinea pig. Short-haired guinea pigs do not require the same regular coat care as that required for long-haired guinea pigs. An occasional light rub-down will remove any stray hairs and stimulate the hair follicles.

An English Crested guinea pig. Note the glossy quality of the coat.

pig is thoroughly dry before grooming it. I usually wait until the following day.

There is a natural parting that runs the length of the spine on long-haired guinea pigs, so follow the flow of the coat on either side of this parting. When you brush or comb out whatever remaining knotting there may be, make sure that you grip the base of the hair shafts close to the body. There is nothing a guinea pig hates more

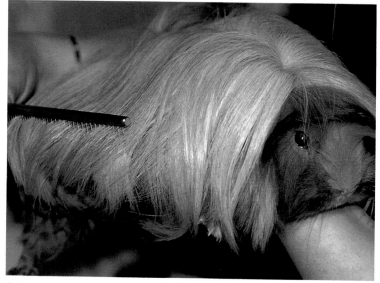

A long-haired guinea pig has a natural parting that runs the length of its spine. When grooming your pet, follow the flow of the hair on both sides of the part.

than having its hair tugged at from the roots. Even the mildest of creatures will turn and take a piece out of your hand if you persist after it has protested.

The degree to which a long-haired guinea pig is trimmed is very much a matter of personal choice, that is unless it is to be shown, when coat length is taken into consideration when awarding points in the judging.

In essence, I restrict

my own trimming activity to the rear end, where I am fairly drastic low down around the genital area, shearing down to crew-cut proportions. The coat tends to hook directly under here and soon becomes soiled. I layer-cut upwards, gradually reducing the amount of hair trimmed off the ends as I go. The hair from about two thirds of the

A Strawberry Roan guinea pig. If you plan to show your pet, he should be groomed to perfection.

A Golden Satin guinea pig.

over the rump. I will do this if the coat is particularly thin or simply if I happen to think this style would suit the guinea pig. Time and experience in making this kind of cut can produce a very attractive rag-mop effect.

I make no apology for my piggy "pomandering" or for advocating hair styles that pander to the owner's taste. I regard such "silliness" as an important part of the bonding between animal and human. The only proviso I make is that whatever a human does to a guinea pig for the sake of appearance, it should in no way interfere with any of

way over the rump is only cut off at ground level, and usually the coat is thick enough to hang down and cover the drastic barbering of much of the rump.

Some people prefer to layer-cut right up

A Peruvian guinea pig. Long-haired breeds such as this can easily soil their coats, particularly their rear ends.

the functions that are essential for the animal's health and well-being.

The key to human-guinea pig friendships is always to handle the animal as much as possible. However, always remember that occasionally you will come across one that simply is not amenable to handling, by the owner or anyone else.

Many guinea pigs try to avoid being picked up, but if they have been handled a lot, they immediately settle down in their handlers' laps. Those that have reached adulthood and, despite much handling, still struggle to get away from humans should have their wishes respected.

I have had three free-range guinea pigs, and only one of them was content to stay for long in my lap. Even his lap time was much less than that of the average penned guinea pig. However, this lack of enthusiasm to be

A Rex guinea pig. The Rex mutation has occurred in other kinds of animals, including cats and rats.

A Lilac Self guinea pig. Keeping your pet clean and well groomed is an important element of good guinea pig management.

handled has always been more than compensated for by the confidence and trust they have shown toward me. The only way I can describe our relationships is that they have always seemed to be more of mutual respect than anything closer. For me, to be respected by an animal is just about the highest compliment I could wish for!

Multiplication

To breed animals to exacting standards is an art in itself, requiring a good grounding in basic genetic principles to achieve successful results.

The first thing to ensure before you breed your guinea pigs is that the surplus offspring have good homes to go to. You will get a vast amount of pleasure out of

Breeding requires forethought and planning. If you don't have the time and resources to devote to a family of guinea pigs, don't undertake such a venture.

A guinea pig mum and her youngster. An understanding of basic genetic principles will help to ensure the success of your breeding goals.

It is a good idea to keep a written history of your breeding stock. Doing so will enable you to select the best animals for pairing.

matching the mating pair, watching them settle in together, and from the wonderful sight of the sow's growing girth. You may even be lucky enough to watch her bring her young into the world, which is as heart warming as it is to watch them suckle from her. Giving her young away without thought for the home they are going to would be poor payment for such pleasures.

Obviously it is important that the animals be in good health and have a good health record in the past. I regard temperament as the deciding factor in any kind of breeding, not only for the ease of handling for the owner but for the overall health of the offspring. Therefore, avoid continuing a scatty or nervous line.

AGE FOR BREEDING PAIRS

The ideal age for a sow to begin to breed is five months and never later than ten months. If a sow hasn't been bred by this age,

The breeding pair should be well grown for their ages and in good condition.

then she should never be bred at all, for she would be in grave danger of suffering from dystocia when she tried to give birth. This usually proves fatal and is caused by the fusing of the pelvic bones, which occurs

In general, most guinea pigs make good mothers, but there are exceptions. If your sow rejects her litter, it might be best not to breed her again.

For many fanciers, breeding is the most rewarding aspect of keeping guinea pigs. It is exciting to watch the youngsters grow up.

by the time the guinea pig is twelve months old.

For a first pregnancy it is advisable to use a young boar, eight to twenty weeks being the ideal. They tend to sire larger litters, avoiding the risk of overlarge

"minipigs," which are more likely to occur in small litters. The litter is usually small in the first pregnancy, two to three being the average. Therefore, it is best to avoid the risk of even less and consequently larger

The temperament of your intended pair requires careful consideration. Do not breed animals that are nervous or high strung.

young. Once the sow has proved she is capable of carrying, delivering and coping with her young, then older boars could subsequently be used.

GUIDELINES FOR BREEDING

Introduce the pair on neutral ground, so to speak. You can use a fresh hutch or even a large box with some hay, with some fresh vegetables and dry food supplied. There is seldom much antagonism between newly introduced breeding pairs, and the fresh food and new surroundings can usually cause sufficient distraction

A Lilac Satin guinea pig.

for what little there may be.

Some boars immediately try to mate a newly introduced sow, while others will content themselves with a purr, a couple of sensuous passes against her, then settle down and not make any really serious attempt to mount her until she comes into season.

Occasionally, a highly sexed boar will constantly try and mate a new partner, who will first run away, then turn and rattle her teeth at him. Seldom will she

Boars are more likely to fight than sows. If a confrontation does occur, separate the offenders.

Guinea pig babies are born with their eyes open and their coats fully haired. Within a few days after birth, they begin to eat solid food.

actually fight him. Instead, she will eventually deliver the ultimate deterrent, which always cools the ardour of a persistent suitor. She simply stops midstride and squirts a fine stream of urine into the face of her ravisher! It never ceases to amaze me, for it always lands bang on target, over the nostrils, sending him coughing and spluttering and wiping his forepaws over his snout!

The sow has a sixteen- to seventeen-day oestrus. To ensure that she is covered, it is advisable to keep

The ideal age for a sow's first-time breeding is five months. Never wait until later than ten months, as serious, often fatal, birthing problems can occur.

them together at least three weeks. Usually it is necessary to keep them together far longer than that, for guinea pigs are not as successful as breeders as are most other rodents.

There is usually a tell-tale sign that a successful mating has taken place. You will find what appears to be a small plug of candle wax lying on the floor of the mated pair's quarters. This is produced by the boar only after he has successfully ejaculated in the sow and is meant to seal in his sperm.

Guinea pigs offer a wide-ranging number of possibilities for variation in colour and hair.

PREGNANCY

The term of pregnancy runs between sixty-seven and seventy-three days. As it is always difficult to determine when the actual conception took place, counting the days is not practical. However, there are a few pointers that can signpost the progress of the pregnancy.

The first sign that we are in business is the sow's increased water upwards. Some guinea pigs grow grotesquely large and even become a little splay legged in the rear, while others just get slightly rotund.

Sows do not object to being handled right up to the time they deliver their young, but do support the abdomen by spreading the hand wide when you lift a pregnant sow.

You will feel a "quickening" (independent movement of her young) a week to ten days before she is due to deliver. Just forward of the vulva you will feel the ends of the pubic bones. Feel them early on so that you will know what to look for when she gets closer to her time.

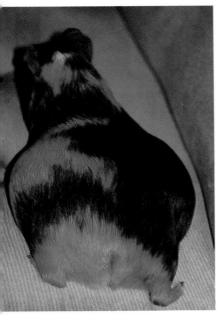

The girth of this pregnant sow indicates that she will soon give birth. The gestation period for guinea pigs can range from sixty-seven to seventy-three days.

intake, at about two to three weeks into her term. Gradually her girth will widen, beginning lower down on her body and then slowly ballooning

A sow assisting her youngster in his grooming efforts. Guinea pigs experience a rapid rate of development.

Three to four days before the birth is expected, they will begin to part. When they have separated to a distance of about half an inch, you can expect the birth to occur anytime during the next forty-eight hours.

During the last three

weeks of her pregnancy, ensure that she gets a daily bowl of bread and milk or a fortified milk-drink of the kind given to convalescents. Continue giving this two weeks post delivery, for it will be beneficial to both mother and young.

Remove the boar as soon as you are sure that the sow is pregnant. This will not only avoid upsetting her with any changes closer to her time but will also be a precaution against another pregnancy and risking her babies! A boar will never intentionally harm his young. However, if they happen to get in the way when he tries to

Even though they begin nibbling at solid food when they are only several days old, young guinea pigs need their mother's milk until they are about four weeks of age.

In general, sound and healthy guinea pig parents produce offspring that have the same qualities.

re-mate the sow when she comes into season a few hours after she has given birth, they may get injured or killed.

BIRTH

More often than not, you will awake one morning to find mother and babies scurrying about their quarters as though they had been there all the time! There may be a bit of blood and the remains of some of the afterbirth, but other than that there will be

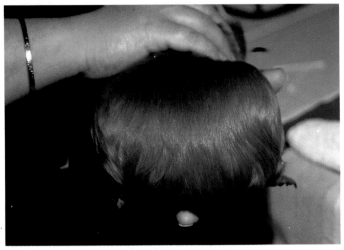

When you hold a pregnant sow, she must be firmly supported under the abdomen to prevent injury to her babies.

no indication that something extraordinary has happened.

Most deliveries go off without a hitch, but sometimes there may be stillbirths or babies that have survived only a few hours. These should be removed from the quarters immediately.

If you happen to be present during a birth and problems do arise, much can be done to retrieve the situation. If I explain what the mother herself does, perhaps it will be an aid to anyone who finds themselves, perforce, to be a guinea pig midwife!

When contractions

An English Crested guinea pig. The better your foundation stock, the better the chances of your producing quality animals.

begin, the sow hunches on all fours, back arched. With each contraction she will lift herself high on her back legs, grunt, then put her head down between her back legs and try to pull the baby out with her incisor teeth. Sometimes she manages this the first time; othertimes she has to make two or three attempts.

Sometimes the babies come out in a rush, while others take a little longer. These are the ones to which the umbilical cord is still attached. The sow will nip through the cord while her head is still down between her legs, though occasionally it will be bitten through when she has actually got the baby out and onto the ground.

Sometimes, the membranous sac in which the baby was carried within her is still intact after the baby has been

Young boars should be housed separately when they reach about one month in age, as they will be capable of mating with their mother (or sisters) at that point.

delivered. The mother will immediately break it by nipping at the head end of the baby. Usually, the baby looks

with her forepaws and knock it quite roughly with her muzzle until it coughs into life. I always equate this action to that of the old-fashioned midwife who used to give newborn babies a hefty whack on their backs to "kick start" them into life.

Sometimes two babies will come out in a rush. These are invariably still contained in their sacs. This is where the owner's intervention is vital, for the mother will usually concentrate all her efforts on just one, totally ignoring the other. I believe that instinct tells her that it is better to save one than risk the

pretty lifeless when the membrane of the sac rolls back over the shoulders. This is when the mother starts to play football with it!

She will kick at it

possibility of losing both by dividing her attention.

Still enclosed in its sac, the baby will quickly suffocate. Therefore, pick it up, put it on a towel and nip the membrane at the head with the finger nails or a pair of scissors. Immediately roll the baby over in your hands a couple of times, quite vigorously, aping the actions of the mother when she plays "football" with a

A sow nursing her young. Note the variation in colour among the babies.

Before breeding a pair of guinea pigs, be certain that you can provide good homes for the youngsters.

troubled baby. Once it has coughed and taken its first breath, rub it in your cupped hands.

If there is no response from your rolling actions, try laying the baby on its back and exercising the back legs by grabbing both feet and pumping the legs up and down, vigorously. As soon as you have the baby up and running, so to speak, return it to the mother. made me dizzy with delight and left a tremendous feeling of achievement. I have failed on one occasion and obviously felt deflated, but you

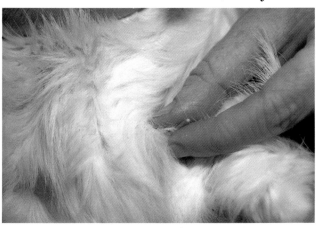

Check the sow's nipples several hours after she has given birth to determine that her milk has come in. If after twenty-four hours it has not, you will have to wet nurse the babies.

I have used these methods several times. The euphoria when that cough came, as the little ones responded to my help, simply cannot win them all.

In cases of single-baby or small litters, the mother may have trouble delivering a

When wet nursing a baby guinea pig, *always* use a spoon. If you use a hypodermic syringe, which is routinely used with adult guinea pigs, the baby is likely to choke to death because it is not capable of synchronizing breathing and swallowing.

large baby. This will be indicated by her constantly straining but producing no baby. Help can be given by lubricating the birth canal with a water-soluble medical lubricant, inserting a little finger and hooking the nail behind the baby's incisor teeth. Traction should be applied *very gently* in conjunction with the mother's

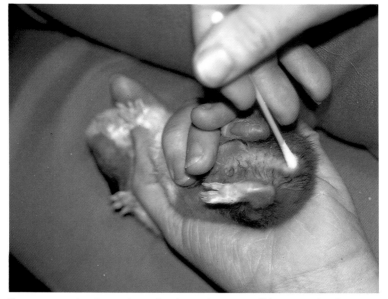

If you are caring for orphaned guinea pigs, you will have to stimulate them to defecate. After every feeding, gently massage the genitals with a cotton bud soaked with warm water.

contractions. Never attempt to pull forward unless it is in unison with these contractions, as this could cause a complete prolapse of the uterus.

You will notice that during all the activity of delivering her babies, the sow will break off now and again to gobble up some of the afterbirth. Some sows eat it all, others just a little, but it is essential that they do eat some, for it stimulates chemical changes that start the process that brings her into milk.

The sow's milk doesn't come on stream until a few hours after the birth. This causes no problems to her young, for they have sufficient nourishment within them to last them for between twelve and twenty-four hours. Unfortunately, this fact and the kindness of some owners have

A Lilac Satin guinea pig. Never breed any guinea pigs that are ill or exhibit any kind of deformity.

caused the death of many baby guinea pigs! These deaths have occurred when owners have taken over the role of wet nurse because either the mother has died giving birth, or because, as happens on rare occasions, she has rejected her young.

Never ever try to feed a baby until it is at least twelve hours old, for it will almost certainly die.

Check to see that the sow has come on stream a few hours after birth by gently squeezing each of her two nipples. If by the end of twenty-four

Because a sow's nipples are low to the ground, the new mother has to hunch her back when nursing her babies. Otherwise, she may suffocate them.

Guinea pigs are not difficult to breed, but you should be prepared for any emergency that might arise.

hours she is still dry or is only "firing" on one nipple, then wet nursing is called for.

While it is a lifesaver to feed sickly adult guinea pigs with a hypodermic syringe, it is fatal to do the same thing with a baby. Not only is the baby unskilled at synchronizing breathing and swallowing, no matter how little the pressure on the plunger, but also the syringe could force too much food into such a little mouth. What usually happens if syringes are used is that some of the food ends up in the baby's lungs, with fatal results.

Caring for a guinea pig family requires time and patience on your part, but the rewards are worth it.

Baby guinea pigs are eager to nurse, but they do not nurse for long periods of time. Don't force them to take more food than they want.

Use a teaspoon, which should be presented level to the baby's mouth, but always be ready to angle it downwards. The babies are usually so eager that they are inclined to stick their noses right in, and the food could get down into their lungs via that route. Any of the reputable non-flavoured, fortified convalescent drinks on the market are ideal, but make a mixture (with warm water) that is a little more diluted than that recommended for humans.

You will quickly

Guinea pigs are energetic little animals, but they do take brief rest periods throughout the day.

discover that most babies like to suckle, not for a long time, but often, so you must be prepared to be available. Never be tempted to force more food on them to enable you to cut down on the frequency of your wet nursing. However, so long as you give them a good feeding the last thing at night, they will be fine until the following morning.

If you have ever seen a guinea pig mother suckle her young, you will also notice that

A Cream Self guinea pig.

Above: Naturally, large litters are more physically demanding on the sow than are small ones. *Below:* The runt of the litter.

A Coronet guinea pig. As a young guinea pig matures, his personality becomes readily apparent.

she spends a great deal of time vigorously licking their genitals. This is done to stimulate them to defecate. This service must be provided by the wet nurse. A cotton bud and some warm water make a good substitute mother's tongue. Roll the baby over on its back and massage the genitals after every feeding. This usually makes the baby produce a pellet or two but not every time.

For far too long, the

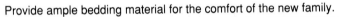

Provide ample bedding material for the comfort of the new family.

Just as with people, old age in guinea pigs can mean physical problems. The Himalayan guinea pig has cataracts.

runts of litters have been considered to be not worth the effort of feeding. These runts are the ones that are well below the two-and-a-half to four-ounce birth weight of a healthy guinea pig. To some hobbyists, they look so frail, with their bony hips and uncontrollable shaking, that by the harsh rules of survival of the fittest they should be left to fend for themselves and inevitably perish.

I myself have owned runts—and seen many other people's runts—that have grown up to be big healthy guinea pigs, and they, in their turn, have sired healthy youngsters. I disagree with the dictum that nature should run its course.

Runts are not, after all, wild animals, so I always do my best to save these "hopeless" cases.

They must be kept warm at all times. At the beginning, feed them by soaking a small bud of cotton wool in warm milk and gently squeezing it at

Dalmatian guinea pig. Sows can be bred up to about three years; boars a bit longer—about four to five years.

Infertility in a guinea pig can be attributable to a number of factors including poor health, heredity, and advanced age.

the corners of their mouths. If they thrive, then you can switch to the normal wet nurse feeding methods. You will not win them all, but those that you do become very special.

The sight of a brood of guinea pigs suckling from their mother is, for me, one of life's greatest pleasures. As her nipples are low down, she has to hunch her back, to avoid suffocating her babies. I've seen many

Above: His mother's milk will meet this baby's nutritional needs and get him off to a good start. *Below:* Runts can grow up to be big, healthy guinea pigs.

A Tortoiseshell guinea pig. Producing a fine example of a given variety has prompted many fanciers to explore the guinea pig show world.

of my guinea pigs hold this position for very long periods of time—in the case of a large litter. In each instance, the sow straightened her back, with a look of relief, only after the last babe left her.

There are a few sows who are extremely blasé about their motherly duties. They will trot off at any distraction, with their little ones hanging on for dear life to their nipples. It always

Like many other kinds of animals, young guinea pigs will seek out the warmth and security of their mother.

amazes me how the little ones manage to avoid being trampled. However, this seems to have no untoward effects upon them, for I have yet to see one harmed by this cavalier behaviour.

If the mother dies or is one of the rare ones who totally rejects her young, the best course of action is to try and get the babies under another lactating sow. More times than not, the foster mother will accept them as her own.

Apart from the fact that a mother's milk is always best, I believe that mother's warmth

A Himalayan guinea pig. The darkness of the markings can vary from one animal to another.

is a vital, life-enhancing force.

However, unless you know a lot of people with a lot of guinea pigs, the likelihood of having a wet nurse sow handy would be pretty remote. Therefore it will all be up to you and your trusty hot-water bottle!

Put the babies in a cardboard box with an end large enough to take a hot water bottle, partitioned off. With plenty of hay to insulate the babies from the excessive heat of the hot water bottle when it's first put in, they will be able to regulate the amount of heat required. As the bottle cools down, they gradually work their way closer to the partition. One filling is sufficient for quite a few hours.

Guinea pig babies are precocious not only by the fact that they can see from birth and arrive wearing their coats but also because they begin to nibble at the food that will sustain them throughout their lives within a couple of days. However, they still need their mother's milk for between three and four weeks. You will know when she is drying up,

Sexing young guinea pigs is not always easy. This is a boar, as evidenced by the dot in the "Y" shape.

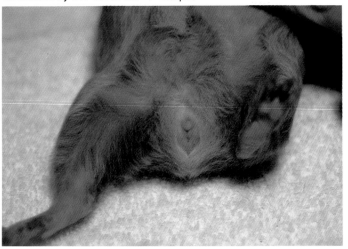

Haphazard matings will likely have disappointing results.

for she will begin to reject them when they try to suckle. This is the time to remove the boars, for they will soon become fertile.

SEXING GUINEA PIGS

I usually sex my guinea pigs when they are about a week old. When the animals are very young, the genital areas of sows and boars are very similar. Even with my good glasses on, I have (and still do) made mistakes when I try to sex infant guinea pigs.

A pair of guinea pigs: a runt and an adult.

Both sexes have a "y"-shaped configuration in their genitalia. However, in boars, a small dot is visible in the center of the "y."

As a footnote to this chapter, I have to state that I am against linebreeding, that is, the mating of closely related animals such as daughters back to fathers, to produce certain characteristics. Though this is a common practice amongst breeders and the fancy, I believe it can cause genetic health problems in the long run.

Linebreeding can produce desired characteristics, but it can also magnify inperfections.

Mending and Minding

Though I have not had any kind of professional veterinary training, some of the treatments I shall be recommending involve the use of "prescription-only" drugs. These drugs can be obtained through a registered veterinary practitioner and should be used only under his or her advice. Additionally, if you are inexperienced in the application of the specific "hands-on"

Below: A Peruvian guinea pig. *Facing page:* A guinea pig about to have its claws clipped. Note how the animal's body is firmly supported.

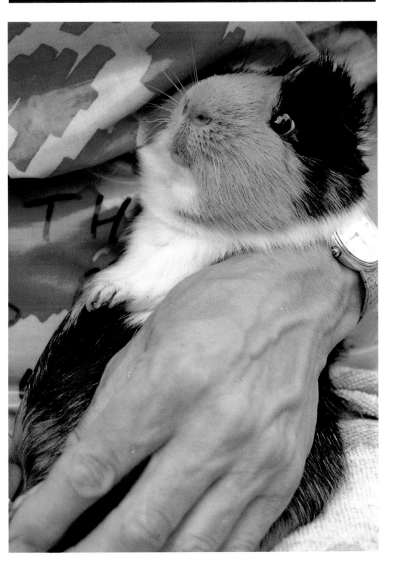

For far too long, the myth that guinea pigs "give up too easily" whenever they fall sick has been wrongly taken as gospel truth by both breeders and some members of the veterinary profession. I mean to make it my business not only to dispel this myth but also to make people aware that they can do far more to care for their sick guinea pigs than they would have dreamed possible.

I shall only be putting forward remedies with which I, or people that I know, have had success. I use both conventional and herbal medicines, most of which are in pill, powder, ointment or liquid form.

A guinea pig that appears ill should be isolated from his fellow guinea pigs and put into a "hospital" area until he is better.

medical procedures that I am presenting, you are again advised to seek the advice of a professional.

Strawberry Roan guinea pig. Note the condition of this animal's coat, which is smooth and even throughout.

Above all, I shall stress the importance of nursing care, for this is the key to the cure more times than not.

SKIN COMPLAINTS

I will begin with the two most common complaints of all, which are fungal and parasitic infestations of the skin and hair. The fungus is called mycoses, more commonly known as ringworm; the parasitic infestation, known as mange, is caused by the sarcoptic mite. The former is more common in stock kept outdoors, for its spores are airborne, but indoor stock can still pick it up. The latter is thought to lodge in hay, before moving onto the guinea pig.

A great deal of

This guinea pig is suffering with an advanced case of mycoses, more commonly known as ringworm. Check your pet's coat regularly and thoroughly. Doing so can help to prevent—or at least lessen the extent of—such a condition.

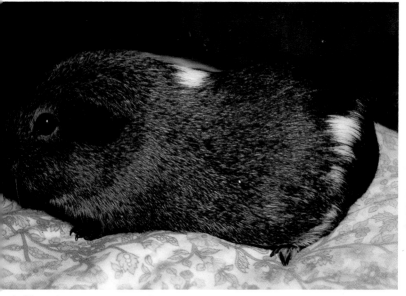

A Silver Agouti guinea pig. Bald patches and sores are things that you have to look out for when you check your pet.

suffering is caused to guinea pigs because of the failure to distinguish the one from the other. About eighty percent of the guinea pigs that I treat for chronic skin complaints have been wrongly diagnosed and treated. I will deal with the more serious condition of mycoses first.

All guinea pigs scratch a great deal, but most of the time this is nothing more

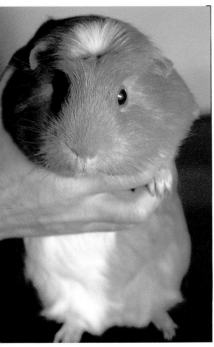

Some guinea pigs are more tolerant than others when it comes to routine health maintenance. If your pet is skittish, make sure that you have a secure grip on him when he is getting his checkup.

then that's the time to pick it up and, as I like to put it, "have a good rummage around" in the coat.

Sit the pig on a towel in your lap. Using both hands, part the hair and really get down to skin level. What you will be looking for are bald patches, any sign of scurfing (similar but far thicker to that which appears on human scalps) and any small lesions caused through scratching.

Rub your fingertips vigorously on the skin surface, and you will notice that many of the hair shafts fall out. It is deep in the individual hair follicles that the spores take root. As the condition

than normal grooming activity. However, if one begins to squeak, irritably, as though it cannot get satisfaction,

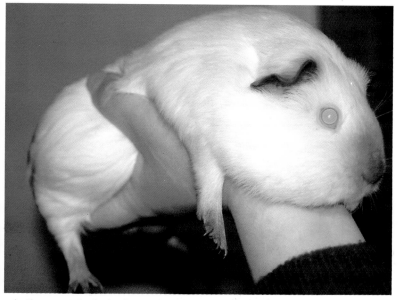

Lethargy and a lack of appetite can be signals that your guinea pig is not feeling well. The more familiar you are with your pet's normal behavior, the better you will be able to detect when he is ill.

worsens, the coat takes on a greasy texture, and hair will come out in thick tufts. This does not happen with mange. It is important that all the loose hair is removed.

The treatment for all strains of fungal infestation is the same. Only the length of the course varies with the severity of each case. The first thing to do is to shampoo the animal in one of the shampoos that are used for seborrhoea in dogs. It is perfectly safe to use this, but like all shampoos, avoid getting lather in the eyes. Work up a good lather, rub well in, then leave the guinea to stand for about five minutes. Then comes the hard part!

You literally have to pluck the guinea pig like a chicken, removing as much of the hair that will

Treatment for mycotic infestation involves several steps. Here, the hair of the afflicted area is being plucked out. This will better enable a fungicide to fully penetrate the skin.

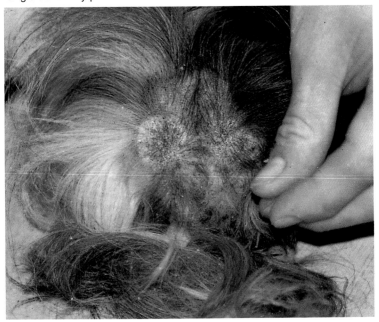

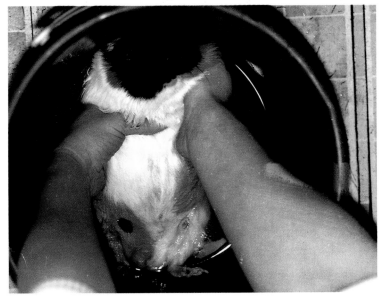

A guinea pig with mycoses being dipped in a fungicide. For this treatment to be completely effective, it should be repeated on the third day following the initial application.

respond to a tug. Needless to say, you will, at times, pull on some well-rooted hair, which will obviously cause the guinea pig some pain. This is unavoidable, for it is essential that as much of the infected hair is removed as possible.

Causing pain in order to heal a pet animal is even more distressing than doing the same thing to a

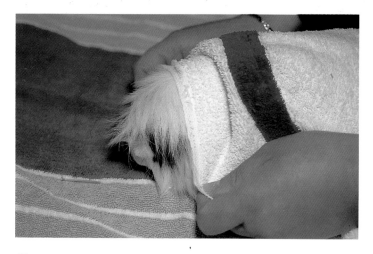

Above and below: A "pig in a blanket." Adult guinea pigs should be given medication via a syringe. Since the "patient" may wriggle or squirm, first package him up—as shown here.

A Dutch guinea pig. A nutritious, well-balanced diet will contribute to the overall condition of your guinea pig's coat.

human, for at least in the latter case you can explain that your "cruelty" is a kindness.

The next part of the treatment is to dip the guinea pig in one of the fungicides of the type used upon cattle. The one I use is Imaverole, which is made up to a fifty parts of warm water to one part of Imaverole solution. Always dip twice, the second time on the third day. Sometimes it may be necessary to give a third dip in a week to ten days after the second dip, to remove some stubborn spots of scurfing. These spots are

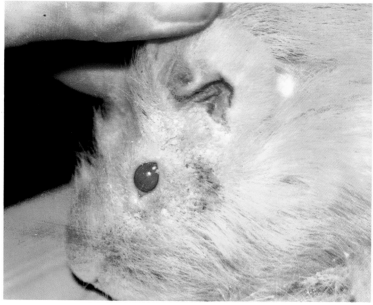

An advanced case of mycotic infestation. In addition to the discomfort caused by itching, this guinea pig is likely to irritate his eyes or his ears by scratching.

usually localized: high up on the back between the shoulder blades, low down on the rump, or under the chin.

If the condition has been detected early, before there are any deep-scratch lesions, if the bald patches are sparse and the scurfing is light, then no more treatment will be necessary. However, if it has taken hold and continues to worsen, then it will have to go

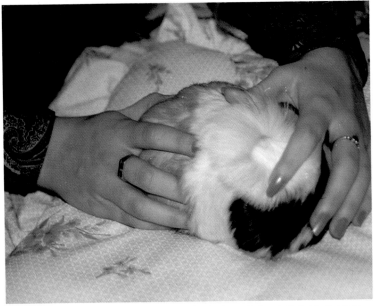

When checking your pet's coat, part the hair and check it right down to the skin. Work in small sections at a time.

on a course of griseofulvin and one of the dietary-supplement oils for skin and coat. Vetrol X and a cod-liver oil specifically formulated for pets are the ones I use.

One word of warning: under no circumstances should you give griseofulvin to a pregnant sow. It can cause deformities in her young. The only course open in these cases is to dip for the time being, and then put her on the griseofulvin treatment after lactation.

The best way to dip is to make up enough solution to fill the bottom of a narrow bucket to a depth of about four inches. The reason I specify a narrow bucket is that most guinea pigs take it into their heads that their owners have suddenly turned nasty and are attempting to drown them! They flounder about in a large bucket, but in a narrow one, they have the side upon which they can gain a

A guinea pig plagued by scurfing, a dandruff-like condition. The flaky segments of skin are thicker than those that are symptomatic of human dandruff.

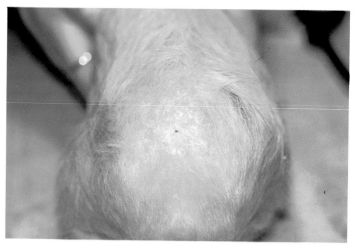

A gentle scratch or massage under the chin will help to relax your pet when you are performing routine maintenance on him.

purchase as they stretch out their rear legs—and consequently feel more secure.

Lower them down into the water on their backs until just their snouts and eyes are above the surface. It is important that the solution gets into the ears, so they must go under as well. There is usually much them soon settle down. I'm not sure if this is out of stark terror or because the warm water has a relaxing effect upon them!

After dipping, just take the guinea pigs out and rub them down with a towel to get rid of the excess water, but do not dry them. Just let them dry out naturally and not with an electric hair-dryer.

The duration of the course of treatment for the more serious cases is three to six weeks. The actual length of time is determined by the healing of all lesions, no reappearance of scurfing, and firmly rooted hair appearing where the bald patches were.

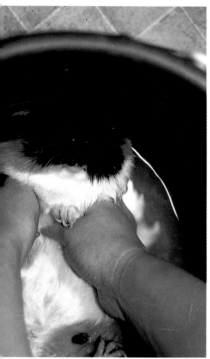

When dipping your guinea pig in a fungicide, do not let the solution get into his eyes or mouth.

protesting—both physical and verbal— from the guinea being dunked, but, surprisingly, most of

The coat of a long-haired guinea pig can be styled in a number of ways. Whichever one you choose, it should be with the comfort of your pet in mind.

In my opinion, putting medicines in water bottles or upon food is next to useless, so the gentle art of "piggy packaging" has to be learned. Place the guinea pig on a flat surface, drop a towel over its back, then pull the forward ends of the towel up around the throat—effectively trapping the forepaws. Scoop it up and roll it onto its back. Bundle it up nice and tight, like a babe in swaddling

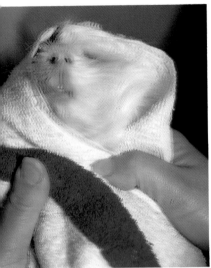

After administering a fungicide dip, blot the excess moisture with a towel, but do not dry the animal. Let him "air dry."

conditions are obtained.

Finally, on the subject of mycoses. There are many strains of this fungus. One of them that the guinea pig is subject to is not species specific. In other words, it is not at all fussy about where it takes up residence: a human being will do just as well! Therefore, the need to thoroughly wash your hands in disinfectant after handling a mycotic guinea pig is vital if the fungus is to be deterred from making a "change of address"! However, it certainly isn't in the remotest bit life threatening to a human being. It is more of a minor irritant.

clothes—with just its head poking out at the top.

Administer the dietary-supplement oil (for skin and coat) at the dose of 0.5 ml, via a syringe. This and the griseofulvin are given daily until the above

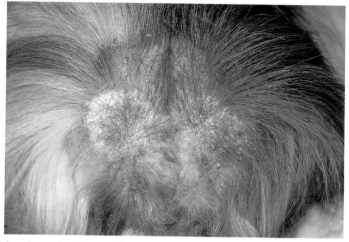

A guinea pig with an advanced case of mycoses. Always wash your hands after handling an infected guinea pig.

MANGE

Mange, the parasitic infestation that guinea pig flesh is heir to, is as common as mycoses but less of a threat to the animal's overall health—and certainly far easier to combat. The guinea pig will scratch a little more than usual. There is a thinning of the coat, leading to a more generalised baldness, rather than the small patches seen in the initial stages of mycoses. There is either no scurfing at all on the skin surface, or what little is evident is light, and more like human dandruff. Sometimes there can be small raised spots on the skin, similar to goose pimples.

The most effective way to avoid this problem is to administer a dose of ivermectin every six months. The dosage is just one drop, orally, then another after a fourteen-day interval. However, this is a P.O.M. (prescription-only medicine), and some vets will not

A Peruvian guinea pig. Long-haired guinea pigs and short-haired guinea pigs are equally susceptible to skin problems.

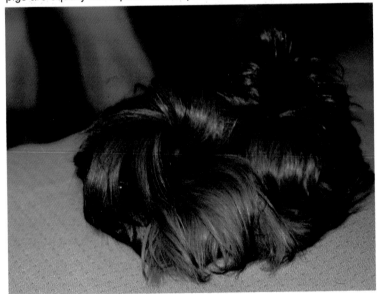

A guinea pig with a skin affliction such as this is as uncomfortable as he is unsightly. Following the basics of good guinea pig husbandry can help to prevent such problems.

supply it as a preventive measure, so be advised that there are alternatives.

There are many products that can be bought over the counter, at a reasonable price, that will tackle parasitic infestation. Additionally, providing you follow the manufacturer's instructions carefully, they are perfectly safe to use. Sprays, shampoos, or dips, they all do the trick. Some external parasiticides have the added advantage of leaving the coat beautifully soft.

It is always advisable to dip any other guinea pigs who cohabit with the one infested, for they could already have picked up the parasite, even though there are no symptoms.

After any infestation, it is a good idea to thoroughly clean out

Crunchy fresh foods such as celery will be relished by your guinea pig. Additionally, they will provide him with the opportunity to work his teeth.

A guinea pig's teeth can grow excessively long and actually prevent him from eating. In severe cases, the teeth will have to be clipped. This should be done by a professional such as a veterinarian.

the animals' living accommodation with a wide-ranging disinfectant.

DENTAL PROBLEMS

I now turn to dental problems because they are the second most common reason for guinea pig patients to be brought to me. I have already stressed the importance of feeding a diet that gives the guinea pig's teeth plenty of hard work to do, to keep them in trim. However, there are times when a guinea pig can go off its food for a while, and it doesn't take very long for the teeth-growth rate to get out of hand. Though the animal may quite quickly resume its normal food intake, the pre-molars may have arched too far over the tongue, and thus they may not be groomed down to acceptable levels. Gradually, the

Mouth sores can develop on their own, or they can be the result of a dental problem. A good dental exam includes checking the exterior of the mouth as well as the inside.

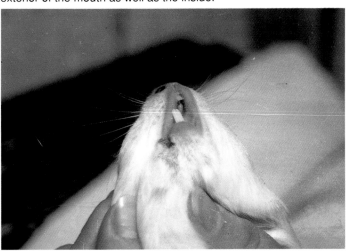

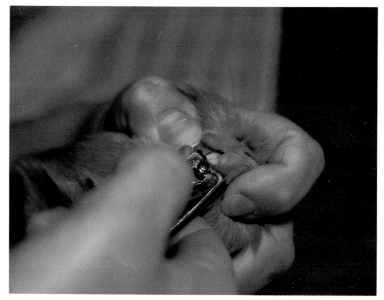

Teeth clipping is not painful to a guinea pig, as there are no nerves in a guinea pig's teeth. Nonetheless, most guinea pigs find this procedure annoying.

essential body-building, high-protein foods, which are usually hard grains or pulses, cannot be handled by the teeth.

There are three very clear external symptoms to watch for, one of them not even on the guinea pig! If you find little bits of its favourite foods, such as carrot or apple, which are usually eagerly devoured at one sitting, lying on the floor of the accommodation, check the teeth.

If the guinea pig seems to be a bit laborious when it is chewing on food, look very closely at the ears! If the teeth are suspect, then they will twitch very slightly, independent of the head.

You may know one of those strange people whose party piece is to wriggle their ears. If you ask them nicely, they will tell you that they do it by gritting their back wisdom teeth together. A similar thing is happening when the guinea pig's pre-molars

Guinea pigs have been known to sustain fatal injuries as a result of a fall. No matter how tame you think your pet is, always have a secure grip on him.

Guinea pigs, be they purebred or mongrel, are generally hardy animals.

overgrow. It has to take a harder bite to make the molars behind the pre-molars meet up properly—hence the ear wriggle.

Thirdly, if the lower incisor teeth appear excessively long and the top incisors begin to curve inward, then this is almost certainly an indication that something is wrong.

Sadly, these early symptoms are sometimes missed, and it is not until the animal has begun to rapidly lose weight that the confirming symptom appears: a constantly wet chin and dewlap, caused by the animal's slobbering.

To prepare a guinea pig for a teeth checkup, towel wrap the animal and hold it firmly in your lap on its back. Hold the jaws open with the index finger and thumb of one hand, then slip the tip of the little finger in over the tongue. About three-quarters of an inch to an inch in, you should be able to feel the tips of the pre-molar teeth of the lower jaw (the upper ones seldom cause

A guinea pig will not willingly submit to a teeth checkup. Therefore, you will have to restrain him. This can be done by wrapping him in a towel and securing him in your lap.

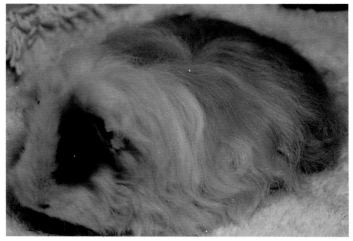

A Texel, one of the newer types of guinea pig. You should be familiar with the signs of a guinea pig that is unwell.

problems).

The gap between the tops of the teeth should be about three-eighths to a half-inch wide. The smaller the gap, the less sharp the teeth feel to the touch, for what you will be feeling are the sides of the teeth as they gradually arch across over the tongue. To give you some measure of comparison, do the same thing with one of your guinea pigs that doesn't have the problem.

There is nothing that you can do yourself, but I strongly advise that you try to find a vet or an expert who can do dental work without the use of an anaesthetic! At the time of writing, I'm afraid they are few and far between. Anaesthetizing guinea pigs carries a high degree of risk and is totally unnecessary in these cases. Therefore, it should be avoided.

There are no nerves in a guinea pig's teeth, and trimming them causes no more discomfort than a human would feel in carrying out the same procedure on toenails or fingernails. The problem is, of course, that the teeth are internal, and the patient doesn't appreciate the need for

There is a wide variety of fresh foods that your guinea pig will relish and that are good for him. (Naturally, you should check that these foods are free of any spoilage before feeding them to your pet.)

the "manicure!"

I have dealt with pre-molars first because they are the ones that, unfortunately, are the more serious threat to the health of the guinea pig if they overgrow. The incisors occasionally overgrow on their own, but the more common problem is breakage, through various means. The usual cause is the guinea pig's jumping, prematurely, from the owner's hands because it had been incorrectly held as it was being returned to its quarters. It stumbles and falls forward onto its nose. On most occasions, it manages to turn its head just before impact, resulting in

A teeth checkup includes the examination of the incisors as well as the premolars.

damage to only one of its incisors—usually in the top jaw but not always. Though I have several specialised surgical cutting instruments, I have found that the best tool for this job is one hold the lips back away from the teeth, cut both teeth together, just below the break or crack. Make sure you use a sharp pair of clippers, and do it with one quick snip, to avoid splitting teeth downward.

Sometimes, the top or bottom incisors will be broken right down to gum level. In these cases, after making sure that the remaining stumps are even, trim the undamaged teeth right back down to about a quarter of an inch. This may sound rather drastic, but if you don't, then they are liable to curve inward, and the guinea pig will be unable to pick up its food.

This guinea pig exhibits every outward sign of good health.

of those large pairs of toenail clippers.

Towel wrap the guinea pig. Then, taking great care to

Even though this Himalayan guinea pig has cataracts, his behaviour is the same as that of his companion.

Naturally enough, after any kind of dental work, eating for a couple of days or so could be a little difficult, so a little bit of help from a "friend" goes down very well. However, do not overdo it and make the guinea pig lazy, for it is vital that it pick up its normal eating habits as soon as possible. This brings me onto the vital matter of supplementary feeding of guinea pigs.

It is a little bit like wet nursing baby guinea pigs, with the added advantages of being able to use a syringe and having a far wider choice of foods. All the foods recommended for the babies can be used. With the aid of an electric liquidiser, almost any item in the guinea pig diet can be fed via a syringe.

The main limitation is the size of the hole of the syringe that is used. Basically, the sicker the guinea pig, the less it wants to waste its energy grinding up food, so the more fluid it should be. Stick to the baby diet or food that can be liquidised fine enough to flow through the small-diameter hole of a 2ml-capacity syringe.

The appetites of the more seriously ill are not as sharp. Therefore, it is better to be able to use a small syringe that can be put deeper into the mouth, to prevent the patient from dribbling the food out.

The more robust patients will take food in larger amounts and of thicker consistency. The 5ml syringes will even cope with the coarse grains of the guinea pig mix when it is liquidised. As you

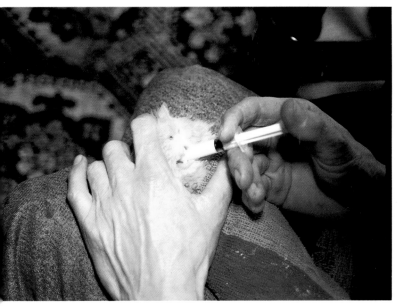

If you have to syringe-feed a sick guinea pig, you can choose from a variety of baby foods, all of which will easily flow through the small hole of the syringe.

can liquidise most of the vegetable matter that a guinea pig eats, this means that you can virtually keep the patient on its normal diet.

Whenever it is necessary to give supplement food, or any kind of medicine for that matter, a close eye should be kept on the state of the pellets passed. If anything makes them loose, then leave it out and try something else.

EYE COMPLAINTS

The two most common complaints are blocked tear ducts and irritation caused by foreign bodies that get into the eye. Some guinea pigs have the tear duct problem more than others, and in these cases it tends to reoccur spasmodically throughout their lives. The symptoms are a watering of the eye and accumulation of waxy or gritty matter along the lower eye lid, more concentrated toward the front of the eye.

Towel wrap the guinea pig, lay it on its side, and put a couple of drops of eye wash on the surface of the eye. If you haven't got one of the veterinary eye washes at hand, any human eye wash will be safe to use. Gently massage the point just below the front of the eye, where the tear duct lies. You can sometimes see the wash suddenly drain away, and the guinea pig will sniffle or sneeze as the fluid travels down into the nasal passages. This is a good indication that the blockage has been cleared, but repeat the procedure a couple of times to give the duct a good flush.

Hay seeds or their husks are the most common foreign bodies to be found in guinea pigs' eyes. This is why it is always a good idea to give the hay a good shake before you put it

This guinea pig is having a hay-seed husk removed from its eye. This problem, which is not uncommon, can occur when a guinea pig rummages about in its hay.

into the pen. The symptoms of this problem are a half-closed or fully closed eye, watering, and, upon examination, red and inflamed muscle tissue inside the lids. Sometimes the eye will remain open, but the whole of the surface of the eye will turn milky and opaque.

Do not be surprised if you cannot see anything in the eye, for more often than not, by the time you have noticed the symptoms, nature has done the job and the eye has been cleared by the actions of the inflamed muscles.

If the husk is still in the eye, it usually lies fore and aft, under the lower eyelid. After

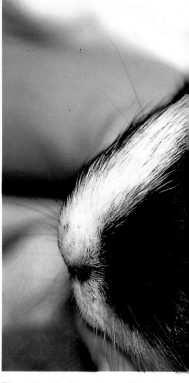

The bulge in this guinea pig's lower eye muscle is evidence of a condition known as fatty eye. It occurs primarily in older guinea pigs and does not cause the animals any discomfort.

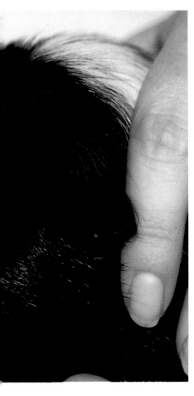

Never pull against the lie of the husk. It would be painful for the pig and could tear the tissue of the eye.

Once the eye has turned opaque, it usually remains that way for two or three days. This is merely nature's way of resting the eye. Moving a "blind" eyeball around is foolish because any damaged tissues repair more quickly through inactivity. A 600mg brewer's yeast tablet for three days hastens recovery.

There is a condition called fatty eye, but it does not cause the guinea pig any health problems—though it may alarm people who are unfamiliar with it. The condition is

determining which is the bottom end of the husk, grip that end with a pair of tweezers and gently slide it out in the direction in which it is pointing.

evidenced by a bulging of the lower eye muscle. It is seen mainly in elderly guinea pigs.

The two main causes of blindness in guinea pigs are cataracts and inherited genetic faults. Why guinea pigs get cataracts is still not known. Many of them develop cataracts as they get older, but some become afflicted when they are only two years old. Sadly, cataracts seldom occur

This guinea pig has a blocked tear duct. Treatment includes the application of an eye wash and a gentle massage to help relieve the blockage.

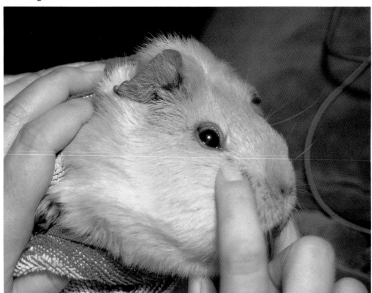

Cataracts occur mainly in elderly guinea pigs, but they can present themselves in guinea pigs that are only several years old. Usually, both eyes of the animal are affected.

singly. One eye is affected, then the other eye usually follows suit within a month. I believe vitamins A and E improve sensitivity to light and shade but only marginally so.

There is nothing that can be done for

congenital blindness, and that includes euthanasia! There is absolutely no reason to put a guinea pig down because it is born, or becomes, blind. I have had, and still do have, guinea pigs that are blind, and unless the eye surface is opaque (thereby advertising their sightlessness), I have to explain to guests which guinea pigs are blind amongst any group of them. To all intents and purposes, they behave exactly like their sighted companions.

MOUTH SORES

These sores are one of those niggling little problems to which

Wounds or open sores on or near the mouth should be treated with a non-toxic anti-fungal agent.

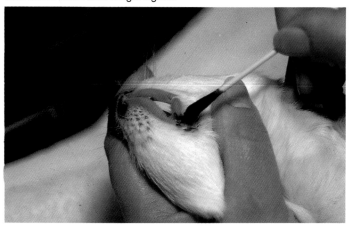

some guinea pigs are prone. Though not life threatening, if not controlled, they can become ulcerous and cause a great deal of pain.

Perhaps, in the majority of cases, it would be more correct to refer to them as lip sores, for most of them begin and end there. It is only when they remain untreated that they tend to spread a little way into the mouth and become localized in the soft tissue just beyond the lips.

The cause could be a vitamin B_2 deficiency so give a supplement in the form of a daily 600mg brewer's yeast tablet. What certainly aggravates the problem

The development of sores in the area of the mouth can be caused by a vitamin deficiency. Such sores can be aggravated by the animal's consumption of acidic foods.

is the eating of any kind of acidic fruit, especially apples. It is possible that the surface of the skin of the lips of those animals affected is a little too thin, or porous, and the acid breaks it down. This would leave the underlying tissue vulnerable to bacterial attack.

The sores begin at the corners of the mouth, then gradually spread along the lips.

It is only after hard scabs are formed (similar to those that form on the site of a human-cold sore) or the guinea pig sometimes squeaks with pain when it has got some hard chewing to do that the owner becomes aware of the problem.

There are two

Any hay that is used for your guinea pig should be shaken to remove husks and seeds, which can lodge in your pet's eyes and cause injury.

An important part of your guinea pig's preventive health care includes routine cleaning of his living area and his food and water utensils.

different remedies for this condition. Usually if the one doesn't work, then the other will, though it takes a little longer.

Gentian violet, which isn't a P.O.M., works in about eighty percent of the cases if the following treatment is carried out to the letter. Towel wrap the guinea pig, then paint the affected area with gentian violet using a cotton bud. Be very careful to keep it off

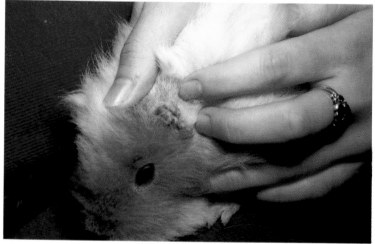

When you check your pet's ears, be on the lookout for a dark, waxy substance.

your hands. Once this gets on your skin, it stains very effectively, and only time will remove it!

The day following the application, and for every day until the lips are clear, remove all the scabbing and apply another coating of gentian violet. The removal of this scabbing is stressful for both the animal and the person doing the work. However, it is a total waste of time painting the scabs, which act as a very effective barrier against the gentian violet's reaching the wound. The good news is that after about the third or fourth day, things

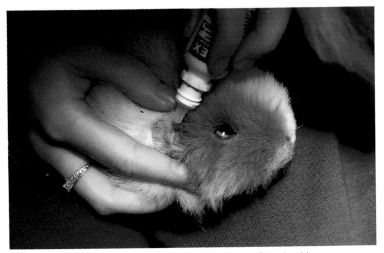

There are various medications for ear infections. Check with your veterinarian to determine which is best for your pet.

gradually improve, for as the sores begin to heal up, the scabbing lessens and does not adhere as firmly to the lips.

If, after a week of treatment, there is no improvement or it looks as though the condition is getting worse, an antibiotic cream is the alternative, and the same routine should be followed as that with the gentian violet.

Continue the treatment for at least a week after all the sores have healed up. In most cases, providing the patient is kept off acidic fruit, they do not reappear. Occasionally, there is not a one-hundred-percent recovery, and in these cases it is necessary to monitor and treat regularly to keep sores within manageable proportions.

EAR PROBLEMS

If the guinea pig begins to tilt its head to one side, it can be one of two things: wry neck or an infection of the inner ear. It should be immediately taken to your vet, who should be able to diagnose the problem. If it is a case of wry neck, then there is little that can be done. If it is an inner ear infection, a course of

Guinea pigs and children are a great combination! Just make sure that your youngster is taught how to correctly hold the animal so that it isn't accidentally dropped and injured.

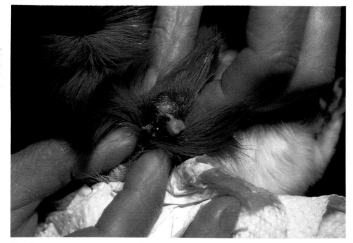

Surface cysts are not as dangerous as those that grow internally, but when they exceed the size of a kidney bean, they can be a problem. Your veterinarian can prescribe the best course of treatment.

chloramphenicol injections are usually successful.

Much ear scratching, or excessive shaking of the head, is usually an indication of mite activity in the ear. There are several products on the market that will deal with this problem. I use a formula of ear drops that is designed for dogs and cats. It never fails to cure the problem. Before using the drops, clean out the ear.

LUMPS AND BUMPS

Let me begin by saying that most of the lumps and bumps that appear under the skin of the guinea pig, though sometimes alarming by their size, seldom seriously affect the health of a guinea pig. However, there is a rider, and that is that their types are identified early on in their development and the appropriate action, and in some cases, inaction, taken!

There are basically three types of these abnormalities: cysts, abscesses and melanomas. The first two can be treated very effectively by vets and experienced owners. Both involve very minor surgery, nothing more than a small incision, at the right time, in the right place, but this is not a job of the inexperienced.

Cysts are the least problematical. They can appear almost anywhere on the body, but the most common site is high up on the rump or just behind the shoulder blades. Occasionally, they can occur internally, in the bladder region. If the guinea pig squeaks a lot when it is passing urine or droppings, then it could be the pressure of a cyst that is causing it some pain. However, it could also be some kind of infection, so it should be checked by a vet.

Surface cysts sometimes reach the size-of a pea and then stop growing, and these I usually leave alone. They are seldom

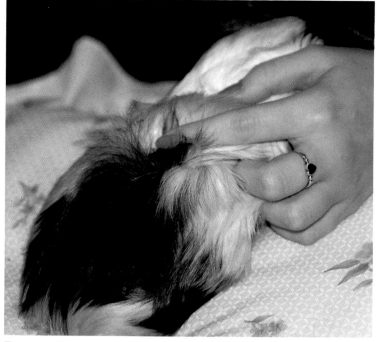

There are three basic types of skin growths that can appear on your guinea pig: cysts, abscesses, and melanomas. They vary in the effects that they can have on your pet.

visible under the coat and cause the guinea pig not the slightest bit of discomfort. However, when they start to grow above the size of a kidney bean, they begin to itch, causing the guinea pig to scratch them. Either by this scratching or because they continue to grow, they will eventually rupture and consequently be open to infection.

The matter inside the cyst, which is not toxic, has to be squeezed out and the cavity cleaned with hydrogen peroxide or some other antiseptic solution. Usually, that is the end of the matter, but some remain active for the life of the guinea pig. These should be monitored and attended to when necessary, but I have yet to hear of one that has caused any serious threat to the overall health of the animal.

Abscesses are more likely to crop up around the neck region, particularly under the chin in the dewlap. They are far more hazardous and painful to the guinea pig. The discharge from them is highly toxic, not only to the guinea pig but also to the owner, if any of it should get into a scratch or cut on the skin. Therefore, the animal should be segregated from any other animals until the abscess has been cleared up, and care should be taken to wash hands after handling.

These lumps are very hard at first. Then, gradually, as they grow they soften—as the contents become more fluid. I certainly do not recommend the old-fashioned hot poultice method of bringing them to a head, on the

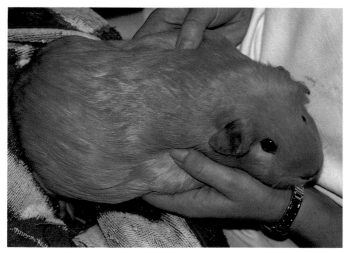

If your pet has a lump or bump of undetermined origin, it is recommended that you take him to a veterinarian for a diagnosis. Don't wait until the condition worsens.

grounds that it is a long and painful procedure. It is best left to ripen in its own time.

As in the case of all undetermined lumps, take the guinea pig to the vet to have it checked. He or she will determine when the abscess is ready for lancing. After this is done, in most cases the incision is left open for a few days to drain out any remaining matter, hence the need to quarantine the guinea pig.

Melanomas come in all shapes and sizes, and in most cases they are usually best left alone. I have seen many a geriatric guinea pig with lumps and bumps all over it that eventually died of old age—not a melanoma. Whereas, I know of many cases in which the guinea pig had a lump that was in no way interfering with its vital functions removed, and it died soon afterwards (the probability being that the lump had been a cancerous one and the surgery had caused it to spread throughout the body).

There remains one lump that can hardly be classified as cancerous. It feels more like a small sinuous nodule, or a series of them grouped together. It can be felt just below the surface of the skin, usually high up on the body, just behind the front legs. However, it sometimes occurs elsewhere. This is invariably subcutaneous fat, and if the animal was a human being, it would be advised to go on a diet!

Guinea pigs certainly do suffer heart attacks, but, in my experience, the fat ones are no more prone to them than the thin ones. All in all, when considering how rapidly a guinea pig loses weight when it goes off its food, even for a short length of time, through illness, I'm inclined to prefer my guinea pigs to be overweight, rather than underweight.

FEET PROBLEMS

Quite a few guinea pigs develop hard patches on the soft, cat-like pads of their feet. Sometimes they can grow outwards toward the side of the foot to form crusty, spur-like projections. I always trim these with a pair of toenail cutters but only if they become so long that they would be liable to snag on something as the guinea pig moves about. I have found that when they are left untrimmed, they are inclined to break the skin at the point where they grow from the pad, leaving a small wound that is open to

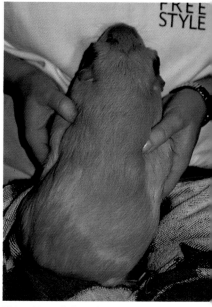

This plump little guinea pig obviously has a hearty appetite. You shouldn't let your pet become obese, but a few ounces over the limit won't hurt.

infection.

The more serious foot problem is pododermatitis, more commonly known as bumblefoot. The initial symptom is a swelling of the foot, which eventually breaks open and becomes ulcerated. Though it appears to contain pus, in most cases it does not, and attempts to squeeze any out make the foot bleed profusely.

This problem is seldom life threatening, but it is extremely painful for the animal, causing it to hobble. It very often occurs when a guinea pig is suffering from a mycotic infestation. When such cases undergo a long course of griseofulvin treatment, invariably the feet heal and resume their normal size. Though this does not work in all cases, I now always recommend a course of griseofulvin.

Whether the success of this treatment is because of the anti-inflammatory properties of the drug, or because it involves, as I suspect, a straightforward fungal infestation, I wouldn't like to say. Suffice it to say that all other anti-inflammatory drugs have failed to deal with the problem.

In cases where pus is found, squeeze out daily, and treat with an oxytetracycline intramammary solution.

IMPACTED BOARS

Before I go on to describe this problem, which occurs in some older boars, I think I should say something

Pododermatitis, a foot ailment commonly known as bumblefoot, is not a dangerous affliction, but it can be painful.

about coprophagy.

Most people are unaware that when a guinea pig bends double and sticks its head between its back legs, it is not always to groom down there but to take some of its droppings for reingesting. Coprophagy, as this is termed, is a perfectly natural function for a guinea pig. Some of the pellets (they are usually smaller and have a glossy sheen to them) have a protein in them that is essential to the animal's health. They are seldom seen because they are usually taken directly from the anus.

When a boar becomes impacted, these particular

droppings, which are softer than those seen lying about the pen, have formed into a solid lump in the peri-anal sac. The overburdened sac can clearly be seen, and, usually, whenever the boar is picked up, some of the normal droppings fall out.

This condition is more common in elderly boars, though younger ones occasionally suffer from it. It is caused by the muscles of the bowel and anus becoming stretched, usually with age. The boar is thus prevented from voiding the softer

A "nose nuzzle" is one sure way to calm your guinea pig and make him feel secure.

Wet nursing a baby guinea pig can be a time-consuming project, but when you see the little creature start to thrive, you'll have a great sense of achievement.

pellets, though the hard ones present it with no problems.

Once more, it is a case of "a little bit of help from a friend." Without this help, the animal will certainly die. It is a very simple matter to take the boar into the lavatory and clean it out over the pan. The job is done by pushing the lump out from behind while rolling back the opening of the anus.

Sometimes, when the lump is exceptionally soft, it is a good idea to smear some petroleum jelly just inside the anus before easing it out. The procedure can sometimes be a bit smelly, and it is uncomfortable, but not painful, for the boar. However, it only takes a few seconds' time.

Occasionally, a boar's health will gradually deteriorate when it becomes impacted, even though it is being regularly cleaned out. This is probably because it is not getting enough of the essential protein it usually gets from reingestion. However, in my experience, these cases are extremely rare. All the boars that I have serviced in this manner have gone on to live out their normal life span.

There is another problem that occasionally crops up with boars, and that is when the top of the penis becomes stuck out of the top of the sheath of skin that encases it. This is caused by dry semen, which literally forms a tight washer around the penis, preventing its retraction. This is by no means restricted to boars running with sows!

If not cleared, the penis can develop open sores and pick up an infection. The semen is usually quite brittle and will break with a slight pressure between finger and thumb, after which, the area should be bathed in warm water. If sores have formed, smear on some antiseptic ointment suitable for animals.

RESPIRATORY PROBLEMS

Whether guinea pigs do, as some people think, pick up colds

Guinea pigs can be afflicted with the same kinds of respiratory problems that trouble humans. In fact, they often exhibit the same symptoms.

from their owners, I'm not totally convinced of, but that they do suffer from the same kind of upper respiratory complaints, there is no shadow of doubt. They present the same symptoms (runny noses, sneezing), but they do not seem to cough as much. Though, in themselves, these colds are a minor matter, I always try to nip them in the bud to avoid any spread of the infection lower down into the lungs.

As a matter of course, whenever a guinea pig shows cold symptoms, always listen to its lungs. This can be done quite easily without a stethoscope. Simply hold the animal up, and press your ear against both sides in turn, halfway down its body. If you hear a "click" in the lungs at the point between exhalation and inhalation, then that indicates a mild infection. If, on the other hand, it is a rasping rattle, then the infection is far more advanced.

As in many cases the lungs are clear and it is a straightforward cold, I'll deal with that situation first. This is where my first herbal remedy comes into play.

For the sniffy nose, I use a decongestant ointment or oil of olbas. A small dab of either product, placed on the nostrils twice a day, usually works wonders, but stop as soon as the nose remains clear for a day. As the mucous membranes are inflamed, each morning I give two pills that basically consist of the essence of nettle, which can be obtained in most herbal shops. These pills are administered orally, through a syringe, after they have been powdered down with a

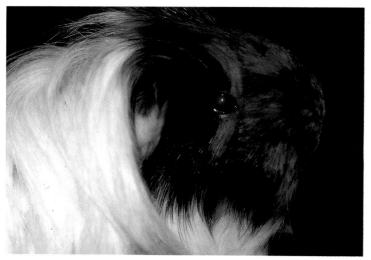

This guinea pig exhibits a condition known as opaque eye. It is actually a healing mechanism, as it gives damaged tissue the opportunity to repair itself.

pestle and mortar and mixed with about 1.5ml of water. Alternatively, they can be placed between some hard paper and crushed with a rolling pin, but a pestle and mortar are more effective and are well worth investing in.

If the infection has reached the lungs, then I immediately turn to conventional medicine. As this involves the use of P.O.M.s (and it is always wise to get your vet to listen more closely to your guinea pig's lungs), it will be necessary to pay him or her a visit.

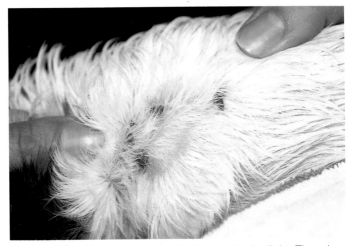

A guinea pig with puncture wounds, the result of a fight. Though they are small animals, guinea pigs are capable of causing painful injury to one another—mainly through the use of their chisel-sharp teeth.

Several drugs are extremely effective in dealing with fluid in the lung: bisolvon, sulfadiazine, trimethoprim and lasix (orally), the dosages to be determined by your vet. A guinea pig suffering from bronchial problems should be isolated from his fellow guinea pigs and kept warm until it is fully recovered.

DIARRHOEA

This is something that must always be very closely watched. In essence, the more fluid the diarrhoea, the more cause there is for concern. An affected

Digestive problems like diarrhoea and constipation can also affect guinea pigs.

animal should be kept in isolation.

A little looseness in the droppings can usually be put right with about 1.5 ml of kaolin and water solution, administered orally. The P.O.M. Kaogel, eight drops twice daily until the condition stabilizes, is also very effective. I regard Bimastat, a P.O.M., as the next stage up, when the droppings are runny but still formed.

If the above does not stabilize the condition within thirty-six hours or the diarrhoea becomes fluid, and especially if the guinea pig fluffs up its coat and sits in the corner, miserable and dejected, then it must immediately be taken to a vet. The condition could be a symptom of quite a wide range of complaints, many of them potentially fatal.

CONSTIPATION

This is something that does not often occur, but when it does, the pellets of the guinea pig are usually hard, dry and a little smaller than usual. Sometimes they come out joined together like a string of sausages.

0.5ml to 1ml of liquid paraffin, orally, usually gets things moving again. This can be repeated on the second day, but no longer, for too much of this is liable to flush out stomach enzymes that are essential to the animal's digestive system. When liquid paraffin does fail and the guinea pig's appetite is poor, then it needs more expert attention.

MINOR INJURIES

If the rules that I have laid down for housing are adhered to, serious fighting should not occur. However, during occasional squabbles, which are common, guinea pigs can nip each other. The fact that the injuries are seldom much more than a puncturing of the skin and that guinea pig blood coagulates very rapidly means that in most

A guinea pig that is not feeling well will not be alert and attentive. Pictured is a Lemon Agouti.

instances owners are unaware of them.

These wounds are usually to be found either on the rump or behind the ears. There will be just a couple of very small scabs, covering two puncture marks. Providing there is no inflammation—and there seldom is—I leave nature to finish off the healing process. On the occasions when the wounds are inflamed, there is usually some pus clearly visible under the skin. Pick off the scabs, squeeze out the pus, then bathe the wound in an antiseptic.

Guinea pigs also suffer from the kind of bruising and sprains that human flesh is heir to. They knock their shins and trip. Sometimes they don't look where they are going and bump into things.

If your guinea pig develops a limp, it is more than likely that it has knocked its shins or fallen awkwardly, spraining a joint. Sometimes, upon examination, you will discover some inflammation at the site of the injury, and the guinea pig will squeak when it is touched.

So long as the guinea pig is healthy in every other respect, I let nature take its course or lend it a hand by giving two nettle pills. Their anti-inflammatory qualities speed the healing process along a little.

Most of the more serious injuries, such as broken limbs, usually occur out of human negligence or accident. The best course is simply to follow the same rules as would be applied in the case of similar human injuries. Keep the patient warm, do not give anything by mouth, and immediately seek professional help.

There is one other condition, which

These two guinea pigs have just received a nutritional supplement. Syringe-feeding ensures that whatever potion is being administered will not be wasted.

appears to be an injury but is in fact a problem of unknown cause, that can occur. This is when what appears to be a perfectly healthy guinea pig will become paralysed in the hindquarters. It happens very quickly, usually overnight, and makes a very sad spectacle. Either the animal cannot move itself around at all or it does so very laboriously with the aid of its front legs.

More often than not, the problem is due to a calcium deficiency, and the cure is to get some calcium into the animal. Give two

300mg calcium lactate tablets, which are available from any chemist, twice a day for the first day, then once a day until the guinea pig is up and about again. While it is immobile, you will have to wash its underside daily, for it will have no option but to lie in its urine. Not only should this be done for the sake of hygiene but also because the guinea pig is a clean animal and would be miserable without this helping hand.

Recovery from this condition, in my experience, has always been complete, and I have known it to reoccur only once. This too responded to the earlier treatment.

PREGNANCY PROBLEMS

If one of your guinea pigs has become pregnant after it is a year old, thereby laying it open to the risk of suffering from dystocia, it can sometimes be saved if it can get immediate veterinary assistance. The administration of 0.2/0.3ml oxytocin in the thigh muscle can be effective, provided the pelvic bones have started to separate. If the pelvic bones remain completely closed, a Caesarean section is the only course of action.

Some sows, especially those in their first pregnancy, abort at about three weeks. This seldom causes them any problems. The only sign that a sow has aborted is sometimes the sight of a little blood around her lips. She will re-ingest the foetus in the same way as she does the afterbirth in a normal delivery.

If a sow becomes listless and goes off her food a couple of days after delivery, she should immediately be taken to a vet, for there is the likelihood that she has developed pregnancy toxemia.

URINARY PROBLEMS

Urinary problems are almost exclusively confined to sows. On the rare occasions when I have come across it in a boar, the same treatment as that

Lifting a pregnant sow. If a sow becomes pregnant after the age of one year, she faces the risks of a difficult delivery.

used for sows has usually been effective.

There are two indications of this condition. One is a

stale odour, making it a simple matter of following your nose to the sow suffering from the problem. The other is a sharp, staccato squeak from a sow that lifts itself on tiptoe when it tries to pass urine. As the infection progresses, the rear end of the underside of the sow becomes sore and begins to lose hair.

One of the best antibiotics for this condition is tetracycline. There are others that your vet would also know about. I have had a great deal of success with nettle pills, twice daily, along with one 200mg garlic pill, also twice daily.

As a footnote, I would add that if there is any sign of blood in the urine, the animal should be taken to the vet. However, don't panic. Though this condition can be indicative of life-threatening kidney or bladder problems, there are many easily treatable conditions that show the same symptom.

For further veterinary information, contact the address below:

Cambridge Cavy Trust
25 Whitton Close
Swavesey
Cambs CB45RT
England
Telephone: 0954-30357

Maintenance and Behaviour

I have included routine veterinary checks and procedures in this chapter because they should be carried out as part and parcel of what I regard as servicing your guinea pigs.

DAILY CHECKS AND DUTIES

Scan the accommodation each morning to see if there are any loose droppings. Also watch out for any small chips of food, carrot

Examining the claws is part of your guinea pig's monthly checkup.

particularly, lying about, indicating the start of a tooth problem.

Just stand for a minute each morning and listen and watch your guinea pigs. You will be listening for any kind of wheezing and looking for limping or listless ones.

As I said earlier, spotting early symptoms can mean the difference between life and death for a guinea pig.

Even if the water bottle is only half finished, flush it out and put fresh water in it.

EVERY TWO TO THREE DAYS

The frequency of bedding changes depends mostly upon the urine output of your guinea pigs. Some produce very little, while others stream in torrents. Some people get concerned about guinea pigs that make much urine. However, only if there is a sudden change from a little to a lot should there be any cause for concern.

If you use shavings, ensure that they are always dust-free and, whatever you use, always put a lining of newspaper on the floor of the accommodation first.

With a long pen-type accommodation, it is best to simply roll back the newspaper, with the hay in it, to about the halfway mark. You

Bedding should be changed every two to three days. You can make the job easier for yourself if you first line the pen with newspaper.

will find that the guinea pigs will become very cooperative, moving down the pen away from the area you are cleaning. With my little lot, as soon as I have put the fresh bedding in the first half of the pen, I simply clap my hands, and they all hop over the half-rolled soiled bedding and root away in the fresh while I'm finishing up at the other end.

With hutch accommodation, it is best to remove the guinea pigs and put them in a cardboard box or travelling case before you tackle the job. A word of warning though, if you have both boars and sows living in separate accommodation. Always clean out the boars' hutch first, or have different "waiting" boxes. If you put a pair of boars into a box that has recently held sows, then there is a great risk of fighting between them. This is especially true when they are confined in a box heavily scented of sows.

WEEKLY CHECKS

By shaking your water bottles once a week—even if you have flushed them out every day—you will notice small flakes of food debris. These collect in the ball valve in the spout of the bottle. Give the bottles a thorough cleaning with bottle and pipe-cleaning brushes.

The most important weekly checks are those on health. It is surprising how quickly they can be carried out. The list of checks sound laborious because I have naturally given the remedies for problems. As most of the time the checks will reveal no faults, it takes about a couple of minutes per guinea pig.

Teeth: Check for any cracks or breakage, inward curving (particularly in the upper incisors), or unevenness in the point where the upper and lower meet. Trim any breakages.

Sometimes you will

see a great amount of hair caught up in the incisors as the result of grooming. Tease these out with a pair of tweezers.

Mouth: Check for any sign of cracking in the lip membrane at the corners of the lips. If any is found, paint with gentian violet and put on B2 brewer's yeast supplement to prevent outbreak of sores.

Eyes: A quick glance will tell you if the eyes are bright and the lids are free of any kind of waxing.

Ears: Some guinea pigs tend to get a greater number of waxy deposits in their ears than others, but check all of your stock. Those that are

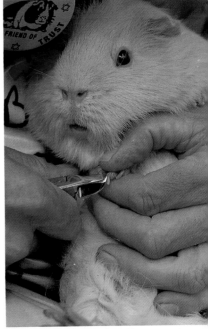

If you are in doubt about how much to clip off of the claws, cut less than more. This can help prevent your clipping into the vein that runs through each claw.

usually wax-free can sometimes get a quick buildup, and they are the ones most likely to pick up mite infestation.

Nose: This should be dry and free of any mucous.

Coat and skin: The coat and skin can tell you a great deal about the health of a guinea pig. Be on the lookout for broken hair shafts, looseness or thinning of the coat, or any bald patches. Apart from mycotic and parasitic problems, these conditions can also be indicative of dietary deficiencies. Is your stock getting sufficient vegetable matter? Have you made any changes in the dry food recently? These are the things to consider.

Watch out for any scurfiness of the skin or any small lesions caused through scratching. Both are symptoms of a developing mycotic or parasitic problem.

It is while you are examining the skin that you will be able to detect any lumps or bumps and be able to take early action.

Feet: Keep an eye on the progress of any "spurring," and watch out for swelling or excessive redness, which could be indicative of the development of systemic mycoses. The redness, of course, cannot be seen on guinea pigs with black pads.

Genital area: With the sows, watch out for any thinning of the hair or rawness on their lower abdomens, which would indicate

Weekly health maintenance also includes a check of the eyes, ears, and nose.

the development of a urinary problem. Check for any inflammation and crustiness of the genital area. Usually, an anti-fungal cream clears things up, but if that doesn't do it, then an antiseptic one will.

Conditions to watch for in boars are dry semen in the genital area and swelling around the peri-anal sac, which could be the start of an impacted anus.

MONTHLY

Check claws. If there is any twisting or if

they are becoming too long, clip them back.

Sit the guinea pig down in your lap, facing away from you. Tackle the back feet first. Sometimes a guinea pig will permit you to do the forefeet in this position as well, but if it is in the slightest bit scatty it will not, and you will have to turn it over onto its back. Things are made a little easier if you wear an apron or have a towel on your lap, and, by opening your legs slightly, make a hollow in which to firmly hold the guinea pig.

If the claws are transparent, cut down to just before quick, the vein that runs down the centre. If they are dark, err on the side of safety. Approximate where the quick would come to, and then allow a little bit more than you would allow on transparent claws.

EVERY TWO TO THREE MONTHS

Shampoo in an anti-parasitic shampoo or human hair shampoo. Some of the anti-parasitic shampoos have pleasant scents, others most certainly do not. As I routinely dip my animals in Tetmosol every couple of months, I always use the same shampoo on them as I use on myself.

Just above the spinal base on the rumps of boars there is a

In addition to checking claw length, you should also look for any claws that are twisted or curled.

scenting gland that produces a soft wax. On some guinea pigs this gland occasionally becomes hyperactive, forming an unsightly and potentially health-threatening patch. As in the case of the ears, mites can be attracted to live off the wax. It can also make the surrounding coat very greasy. I have found grease solvent, the type used by car mechanics, to be a very effective cleaning agent and perfectly safe to use. There appears to be a two- to three-month cycle when even the boars that produce hardly any wax still need this treatment.

I find that my long-haired varieties need their rear ends trimmed about every two months. The hair along the flanks seldom needs trimming because the guinea pigs tend to flick it upward, off the ground.

A word of warning: Always cup a boar's testicles in your hands when trimming his rear. I didn't, once, and one of my favourites had a very close shave indeed. It cost him four stitches and a great deal of soul searching on my part!

Keep a record of the health of your stock. It will be very helpful when problems do crop up.

GUINEA PIG BEHAVIOUR

When it comes to the subject of the behaviour of guinea pigs, it must be remembered that all my conclusions come from living with indoor stock. Consequently, my presence is likely to have some effect on the patterns I have observed. My guinea pigs certainly have an effect on the patterns of my own behaviour! However, I think there is a basic kind of social behaviour that is common to all guinea pigs.

There is definitely a pecking order, even between two guinea

Guinea pigs have a body language all their own. A guinea pig that turns up its head to one side and squats on its haunches is signaling appeasement.

pigs, but it is not as easily defined as it would be in, say, a pack of carnivorous animals. I don't think it can be, because guinea pigs do not have to hunt for their food, an activity that requires a more disciplined social structure.

"Boss" pigs are not necessarily overtly aggressive, but all the ones I have come across have been a little on the wild side, not very amenable to human handling. However, whenever one of my boss pigs has been pushed to the limit, she has always been more than capable of handling herself very well. I get the impression that a boss pig is loath to resort to physical sanctions to impose her will, which just has to be a plus for any leader!

In the domestic situation, it is the little things that mark out a boss. It has to shoulder-shove and bottom-bump its way to the food trough with the rest of the tribe—there are no privileges there. However, once it gets a portion of food in its mouth, no other pig will attempt to snatch it away. Whereas between the rest of the tribe, tugs of war over a dandelion leaf or portion of carrot almost seem to be part of the digestive process. I suspect that is a matter of "stolen" goodies tasting far nicer!

One of the favourite sports of guinea pigs is what I call "berth bagging." By this I mean the practise of ousting a sleeping guinea pig from its berth and taking its nicely warmed spot. This is something that never happens to the boss pig.

I have never seen a boss pig intervene in a squabble between two of the tribe. However, if they happen to have their disagreement close to her, she will raise her head,

There is a definite pecking order among guinea pigs, but it is more subtle than that of some other kinds of animals.

threateningly. The pair will immediately cease and either run away into different corners of the pen or shuffle about from foot to foot like a pair of school children caught in some kind of mischief. Any of the other tribe members will always distance themselves from a tussle, either by pointedly turning their heads or showing a clear pair of heels.

The head-turning is all part of the body language, along with the characteristic vocalization for which guinea pigs are renowned. Thus, harmful aggression is kept within bounds. As guinea pigs give plenty of clear signals about what their intentions are, misunderstandings seldom occur.

Animals are well aware of the futility of combat, and most give signals in an attempt to avoid it. In my opinion, guinea pigs have got this off to a fine art.

A head turned up and to one side, as the guinea pig squats on its haunches, signals appeasement. However, if the head is level, making eye-to-eye contact, or slightly raised but facing head on, while the guinea pig is standing four square to any other guinea pig that challenges it, then trouble is brewing.

The next stages sometimes follow in quick succession, but more often than not, they are slow and ritualistic. The hackles rise, and there is a deep purr, similar to that given when a guinea pig is courting another, but more vibrant. The proponents duck and weave, slowly, but threateningly.

If neither turns its head and breaks off the engagement by shuffling sideways and away, they will eventually fly at each other with amazing ferocity. However, more often than not, one of the warring parties will back down, and the other one will seldom pursue the matter.

In general, sows live peacefully with each other. However, if you encounter a sow that is aggressive with her companions, she should be housed separately.

Then the pair will prowl around the pen, purring aggressively. More often than not, it all peters out.

Most sows get along well enough together, but it is up to the owners to ensure that the relatively rare antagonistic ones are housed on their own.

Unfortunately, accidents can happen. I once put the wrong boar in a carrying case and warfare immediately broke out. I made the classic mistake of putting my hand in and took it out with a guinea pig hanging onto one of my fingers, its incisor teeth firmly locked on one of my knuckles! It made my eyes water, somewhat, and it taught me a good lesson. Throw something over combatants: ideally, a towel, blanket, or a coat, which will immediately confuse them, causing them to break off. If there is no material at hand, then try water!

The most harrowing kind of guinea pig behaviour is when a recently weaned young sow takes up residence with a single adult sow or a group of them. For the first day or so, the youngster will be harried unmercifully by the adults. There are never any warnings of these seemingly senseless attacks, which are frightening in their ferocity. I think therein lies the clue to what they are all about.

At first I used to think that it was all about the pecking order, putting the new comer in its place, so to speak. There may be an element of truth in this, but I think the real reason is a throwback to the guinea pig's wild past.

Baby guinea pigs are very tame while they are with their mothers, but that part of their lives is so short that there is little opportunity of their learning the survival ropes. Such tameness in the big outside world, if maintained,

A lovely Sheltie guinea pig. Guinea pigs that are housed indoors are likely to be more companionable than those that are kept outdoors.

could quickly prove fatal. A guinea pig's survival in the wild depends upon its ability to keep all of its senses on maximum alert—while it goes about its business.

What I think is mainly happening during these attacks on a young guinea pig are lessons in survival techniques. It is, after all, in the interest of the pack as a whole that its new members should conform. The immediacy of these attacks and the fact that they are unheralded—not usual behaviour in guinea pig social etiquette—

mimic just how a predator would fall upon a nice, plump, unsuspecting guinea pig!

"This is how they are going to come at you, `little one.' Shift your backside out of it, P.D.Q.!" seems to be the message the adults are trying to put across.

The reason I believe this to be the case is that the faster a young guinea pig adopts a more defensive approach to life, looking alert at the approach of any adult guinea pig or scurrying for cover when the owner comes near, the quicker the harassment ends.

The good news is that during all the time I have owned guinea pigs, I have never seen a young guinea pig harmed during one of these encounters. From the noise and fury of these attacks, it sounds as though nothing short of homicide is taking place, but this only lends credence to my theory. The rest of the pack immediately goes into "action alert" mode, just as they would in the wild if one of their number was screaming because it was being taken by a predator. However, this only continues during the first hour or so of the arrival of the young one. Presumably, by this time they have come to recognise the alarm squeaking for

Each variety of guinea pig is appealing in its own special way.

what it is: all part of the training programme!

If there are two guinea pigs in a pack that do not get on very well together, they studiously avoid one another. They pointedly turn their heads when they meet and try to give each other as wide a berth as possible. I think this is because guinea pigs are not naturally belligerent, and there seems to be no kudos gained from fighting prowess.

There are squabbles, more so between groups of sows than pairs of sows or boars. However, I believe this to be a very necessary safety valve that relieves the tensions that always occur between animals that live communally. We have only to look at our own behaviour to understand this!

These little spats, which involve one guinea pig's giving what I term a "chin butt" to another one, are usually unheralded, but they are not meant, nor taken, seriously. The fact that puncture wounds from such behaviour are extremely rare underlines the low level of the aggression. The incisor teeth are extremely powerful weapons, but on these occasions they are not used. This is why I use the word "butt" instead of "bite."

There is one type of guinea pig behaviour that leaves me and all the other people I have met who keep these animals completely at a loss. I have read many books about guinea pigs and only one mentioned this behaviour. The writer was as puzzled by it as I am.

There is an ethereal quality about it. Not only do I sense this but also the guinea pig in whose company this phenomenon takes place senses it as well.

Out of the thirty-seven guinea pigs I own at the time of writing, only two exhibit this strange behaviour. From what I

Observing a guinea pig and his reactions to various stimuli is an interesting and educational aspect of the fancy.

have been able to find out from other owners, they too say it was always confined to one specific animal.

The guinea pig will usually be sitting on its haunches and begin to make a slow, pulsating "ha! ha! ha!" sound as it expels air from its lungs in short, sharp breaths. The sound is very quiet at first but then becomes more pronounced. The vocal chords are brought into play as the "utterances" turn into high-pitched squeaks, still at the same regular timing. It is then that any other guinea pigs in the vicinity immediately cease what they are doing and look towards the "squeaker" with an air of what I can only describe as puzzlement and awe.

The eyes of the squeaker are fixed, and it doesn't appear to be aware of anyone else around it, or the effect it is having on them. I once picked a guinea pig up while it was in one of these strange "trances," and it immediately stopped. However, as soon as I put it back down, it seemed to continue where it had left off. Other people have told me the same thing happened when they had intervened. It is as though whatever it is that makes a guinea pig behave in this way has to run its full course.

The trance, for want of a better word, usually breaks off quite abruptly. On most occasions one or two of the guinea pigs close by will go and sniff at the squeaker. I get the impression that they are checking to see that it is O.K.

I have never seen a boar do this, but I have never owned anywhere near as many of them as I have sows, which means that the odds of getting a relatively rare squeaker are just that much higher. Therefore, I cannot conclude that boars never act in this manner.

So, I end with an enigma. Perhaps as a result of this book, someone will be able to give me the answer. If he or she does so, I shall be very grateful, for the more I learn about these delightful creatures, the more I want to learn. I shall also probably gain a new friend, for people who love these animals tend to like others who share their passion for them.

I love all animals, but there is something about a guinea pig that has captured my soul, and many other people's souls in a way that other animals cannot.

I repeat my warning that these creatures are quite capable of causing serious "addiction" on the part of the owner. The symptoms are usually deep contentment and

The guinea pig possesses a unique charm that has won the hearts of many people all over the world.

an absorbing interest that grows in direct ratio to the number of guinea pigs that come into your life!

Index